Favorite Child
a collection of select poems
from all of my books

by

Ann Christine Tabaka

ATC

Poet
&
Writer

Website: https://annchristinetabaka.com

Cover design: Carl Scharwath

Publisher contact: Editor@transcendentzeropress.org

ISBN: 978-1-946460-58-5

This book is dedicated to all writers and poets who put their lives and emotions on paper to share with the world.

watercolor, ink, & Prisma Color Pencil painting converted to B&W image by Ann Christine Tabaka, reduced in size

All of the artwork in this book has been reduced from full size paintings and illustrations. My illustrations were 16" X 22" and my paintings were 22" X 28".

Cover Design by Carl Scharwath
Cover Photograph of Ann Christine Tabaka by Karl Blom (husband)
All Internal Art &Illustrations are original works by Ann Christine Tabaka
All Photographs aretakenby, or are personal property of Ann Christine Tabaka

watercolor paintingconverted to B&W image by Ann Christine
Tabaka, reduced in size

Other Books by Ann Christine Tabaka

Overcast Mind -*My life in poems*

It Is Still Morning - *A Continuation of my Life in Poems*

When Dragons and Angels Collide – *Haiku& Senryu*

Everlasting - *A Lifetime of Poems*

The Sound of Dragonfly Wings - *Haiku & Senryu*

Reaching for Dawn - *Poems*

Just Breathe - *Micro-poems*

No More Hallelujahs - *Poetry chapbook*

Words Spill Out - *Poems*

Keep Breathing - *Micro-poems*

Running Backwards in Time - *Poems*

And Still I had these Dreams – *Poetry chapbook*

Pondering the Shoreline of Existence – *Poems*

I No Longer Hear You Sing – *Poems*

The Lane is a River *and other short stories*

Learning to Climb the Mountain – *Poems*

How Do You Uncook An Egg? –*Poems*

Prologue

"Favorite Child" is a collection of many of the poems that are special to me. They are selected from my previous books - starting from the very beginning of my journey.

I have often said "One cannot choose a favorite child among all her children." I doubt that I could choose just one favorite poem, but over the years, I have found that there are always those few poems that have a cherished meaning for me. They may be about a personal life experience, or a new style of writing that I felt particularly good about.

Since I began playing with words, I have moved from rhymes and musings into places of deeper contemplation. I hope that I have grown along the way. This book is the accumulation of a lifetime of emotions and experiences. I hope that it may intrigue you to further explore some of my older books.
NAMASTE!

Contents

Chapter 1

Overcast Mind
(my life in poems)
My early writing journey from 1966 -2016

pen & ink illustrationby Ann Christine Tabaka, reduced in size

The Cat

A shadowy figure emerges from the darkness
Blessed as well as cursed
Both god and demon
Ancient in his wisdom and strength
He knows all, yet reveals nothing
He is feared and loved in the same breath

Looking out from his place of hiding
He carefully surveys his domain
He is a perfect combination of beauty and grace
All who know him praise him for his affection
Those who do not understand him call him aloof

He leaps to a high place
Stretches slowly, then perches regally
He is magical and mysterious
No other animal has caused so much controversy
Since the dawn of man

He purrs softly and curls up for a nap
In the rays of the newly risen sun
You either love him or hate him
But none can be indifferent towards …
THE CAT!

©1978
(from my book **Overcast Mind**)

pen & ink illustration by Ann Christine Tabaka, reduced in size

The Dream

I had a dream,
White roses, gray smoke.
First there was silence,
Then I awoke.
I had a life,
Dark shadows, cold rain.
For all I could see,
Nothing to gain.
I have love now,
Warm breezes, cool stream.
The silence now broken,
Once more I dream.

©1978
(from my book **Overcast Mind**)

pen & ink illustration by Ann Christine Tabaka, reduced in size

Forgotten

She stands on the corner,
Cold lonely, lost, forgotten;
As her youth slowly slips away.
She hides behind the makeup,
And clothing of her former years.

She evokes a look of pity from all who pass by.
Behind her mask,
Her features show the beauty of her age.
But she refuses to accept this,
And so, continues to disguise her true worth.
Trading it in for a few more years of fantasy.

Why does she cling on so desperately,
To the worn pages of past times?
She has much more to offer now.
Many of us are obsessed with holding on,
To what we cannot have.
And in doing so neglect to see the satisfaction,
That each new age holds out to us.

She mistakes the glances of sympathy,
For admiration.
So, for the moment she is content.
Then once again, all too soon …
She stands on the corner,
Cold, lonely, lost, forgotten …

©1978
(from my book **Overcast Mind**)

My Two Lovers

The morning sun shines
brightly through the window.
My lover lifts his head from my shoulder
and softly nuzzles me.
Swiftly he is gone
without a word.
He stretches in the sun's warmth
oblivious to what events the day may bring.
He does not bother himself with such details;
he knows his needs will be met.
As he yawns and rolls over
to continue his nap,
he purrs.
How I envy him sometimes.
My lover does not know
I have been unfaithful.
He is unaware of the world outside his door
where the red-haired gentleman
waits for me each morning
wanting only a moment of my time and affection.
Life is not taken for granted
out there in the real world.
How very different my two lovers are.

©1986
(from my book **Overcast Mind**)

sketch by Ann Christine Tabaka

22

Dew Drops
(Saturday morning, day break, on the porch)

Drops
of water
on the screen.
Crystal
mirrors
of life unseen.
Prisms
of pure color
bright.
Sunlight
dances
with delight.
Whispers
let your soul
take flight.

©2004
(from my book **Overcast Mind**)

It Is Still Morning

It seems as if ages have passed
since the sun peeked above the horizon.

Since its first warm streaks of amber
graced the early dawn sky.

I sit and wonder as I watch the shadows
grow shorter with each advancing hour.

... But, ah yes, it is still morning.

How slowly the hours pass
now that I am alone with my thoughts.

I watch as each small flower bends its head
and turns its face to the sun.

Surely it must be time to move on
to new places unknown.

... But, ah yes, it is still morning.

The day presses on in endless hours
and time passes in single heart beats.

Soon it will be time to make new plans
but I am stuck in some timeless loop.

It must be hours since I awoke
and forever since the sun first rose.

... But, ah yes, it is still morning ... forever morning.

©2014(from my book **Overcast Mind**)

Tapestry

Leaves swirling
Spiraling down
Tumbling ever
To the ground
Colors dancing
On the wind
Patchwork carpets
To begin
A metaphor
For life and death
The beauty of which
Takes my breath
Spreading forth
For all to see
Mother Nature's
Tapestry

(from my book **Overcast Mind**)

Everlasting

Oh, so many years ago
As I walked upon this land
I did witness many wonders
Wonders countless as the sand

For I am an ancient soul
I transcend both time and space
It has been many eons
Since I came upon this place

The stars above are family
I wear the night as my cloak
I roamed this planet since its dawn
Before man ever spoke

The forests are my castle
The mountains are my throne
Where I oversee the oceans
From which all life has grown

My words have painted pictures
In the minds of those who heard
My voice gives flight to dreams
That soar high as a bird

There are angels in my future
There were dragons in my past
Many worlds will spring forth and die
Before I leave this life at last

I swam with creatures of the deep
And to the moon I gave birth
Within your hearts you know me
I am the spirit of the Earth.©2015

Whisper

Beyond the very depth of your soul
Lies a place where truths are hidden
Where thoughts whisper louder than words
And speaking them is forbidden

There emotions play hide and seek
Among the cobwebs of your sorrow
But love whispers from deep within
Bringing with it hope of tomorrow
Can you hear the whisper?

©2015
(from my book **Overcast Mind**)

Art Deco Design by Ann Christine Tabaka

Winter at Daybreak

Venus, the morning star, is still visible in the sky
as I step outside.
The bright sun breaks through the cold crisp morning air.
My breath drifts heavenward, floating on a cloud of mist.
I watch as it dissipates into wisps of fine vapor.
The cold embraces me and I shiver,
for a moment.
Then I stop and look around me.
I take in all the beauty of that winter morning.
Frozen moisture encases every branch and twig.
It is as if I happened upon a magical wonderland,
where everything is made of glass.
Where sparkling crystals hang from every tree.
The cold no longer has a hold on me,
for I am warmed by all the magic that surrounds me.
I continue on with my day,
taking with me all the wonder that this morning has
presented to me.
My heart soars.

©2016
(from my book **Overcast Mind**)

sketch by Ann Christine Tabaka, reduced in size

Chapter 2

It Is Still Morning
(A Continuation of my Life in Poems)
2017

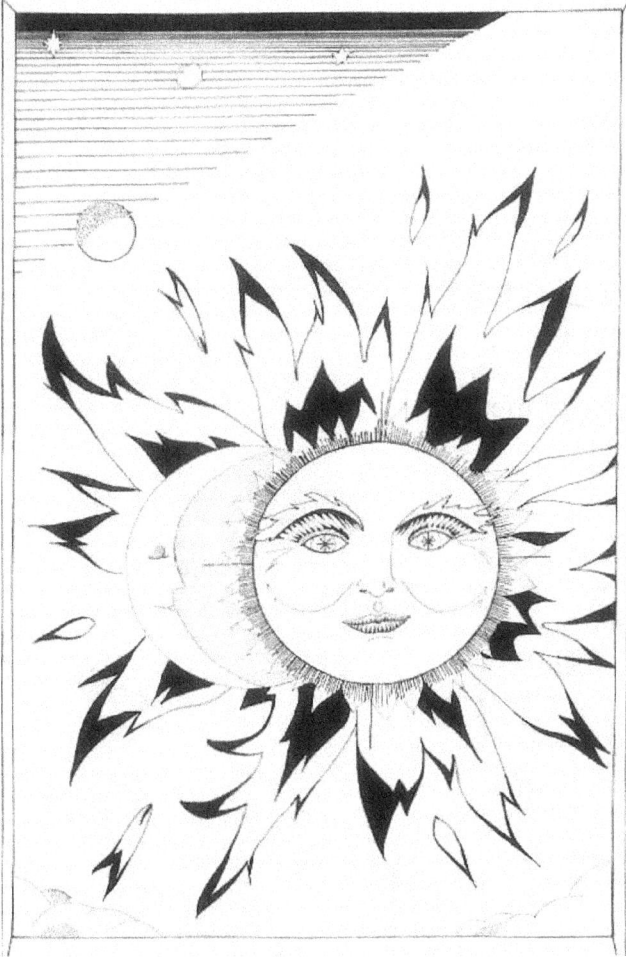

pen & ink illustration by Ann Christine Tabaka, reduced in size

We Are Shadows

As evening falls
Shadows lengthen
Receding into night
They are consumed
By darkness
Only to return
With the rising
Of the sun
Their cycle begins
Yet anew
As they slowly grow
Then once again
They begin to fade
When the sun
Reaches its zenith
The cycle of life
Continues on
Day after day
Never ending
Until that day
When the sun
Shines no more
We are shadows
We live for the light
The very shape
Of our existence
Is dependent
On the light

©2016
(from my book **It Is Still Morning**)

Imagination

The fog closes in
It surrounds me
It dampens my senses
It impairs my vision
But at the same time, it enlivens me
I feel a tingle of excitement
I am transported to another time
To a distant shore
Into a story I once read
Where ships traverse dangerous waters
While lighthouses atop craggy rocks guide them
Back to a time of sea monsters and damsels in distress
A time of mystery and wonder
But then the fog begins to lift
And I must come back to earth
But just for one moment
Time stood still and the fantasy was real

©2017
(from my book **It Is Still Morning**)

sketch by Ann Christine Tabaka, reduced in size

31

Adventure Story

She walked upon the moonlit shore
The same path many had walked before
The air was cold the stars shone bright
As she walked alone that winter night

The wind whipped froth upon the waves
Souls of pirates restless in their graves
Ghosts of many ships of yore
Followed her on that lonely shore

In her imagination she devised a tale
Upon those pirate ships she would sail
Then she would cross all seven seas
As she sailed upon the ocean breeze

But then the sun began to rise
As her dream vanished before her eyes
She vowed to return the very next night
As her fantasy was now a story to write

©2017
(from my book **It Is Still Morning**)

Standing on the Edge

Standing on the precipice
Flying into the sun
Wondering about my life
When my days are done

Spiraling out in endless circles
Like a stone cast upon a lake
Images flash before my eyes
Are they real or are they fake

Once I cross that river
And pay Charon his toll
What will remain of my work
When I am a wandering soul

©2017
(from my book **It Is Still Morning**)

*(Charon - the ferryman of Hades who carries souls of the
newly deceased across the rivers Styx and Acheron that
divided the world of the living from the world of the dead)

Two Brothers

Two brothers
Very different
Yet of the same blood
Raised in the same manner
Nourished with the same love
Yet the paths they take differ so
One chooses a life of service
And the other a life of despair

Two flowers
Very different
Yet started from the same seed plant
Planted in the same soil
Watered and fed exactly the same
Yet they grow so differently
One thrives and blooms
And the other withers away

Two raindrops
Very different
Yet born of the same cloud
Held adrift by the same air mass
Composed of the same elements
Yet they develop into different entities
One falls softly as cold rain
And the other freezes into hail as it descends

There is something deeper at play here
Something stronger than genes and surroundings
Even with the same experiences
Life grows and changes
And there is something inside every living thing
That allows it to become an individual
Call it a spirit, character, nature, or essence
All things will become what they are meant to be in the end

©2017
(from my book **It Is Still Morning**)

sketch by Ann Christine Tabaka, reduced in size

The Rest is Silence

I screamed and no one heard
I cried and was ignored
Just like an injured bird
Whose wings no longer soared

I pled to deafen ears
That did not hear a word
In the pain of countless years
No compassion had been stirred

I asked and no one answered
The questions of the heart
The silence was like a cancer
From which I could not depart

©2017
(from my book **It Is Still Morning**)

Dying Muse

Not everyone will survive
The muse has sung her last song
The end is about to arrive
It has been following us all along

The forest is groaning in pain
She sheltered her creatures with love
Her labors were all given in vain
Of her plight she knew not thereof

The muse is now silent and sad
So let us stop for a moment and cry
She pines for the beauty she once had
As Earth breathes her last mournful sigh

©2017
(from my book **It Is Still Morning**)
This poem is dedicated to everyone who is dealing with
dementia, their own or a loved one:

Nonsense Rhyme
(or/ Dementia Creeps In)

Blue sequins
On the floor
Counting pennies
Like before
Someone knocking
At the door
Seeking answers
They implore

Day one
Is now day two
I cannot
Find my shoe
What am
I to do
The sequins
Are still blue

Time passes
Lives change
Memories
Rearrange
Everything
Seems strange
Counting pennies
For change

Silly verse
Crazy rhyme
Makes sense
In time
Pennies now
Are a dime
The sequins
Still are mine

©2017
(from my book **It Is Still Morning**)

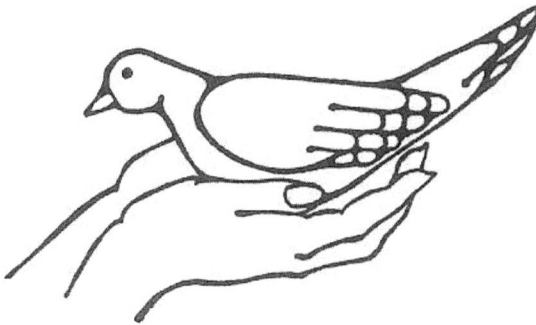

sketch by Ann Christine Tabaka, reduced in size

The Moon Wore a Rose

She wore a red dress
That fit like an embrace
It draped to the floor
And flowed with grace

Ebony hair cascaded
Over her shoulders bare
Her skin porcelain white
A flower most fair

The light she emitted
Was as soft as a kiss
Evening surrounded her
With shades of bliss

She walked on air
As if in a dream
Stars sparkled about her
She was all agleam

One perfect night
Of light and shadows
I will always remember
When the moon wore a rose

(from my book **It Is Still Morning**)

Sleepless

Cold dark nights
I cannot sleep
Minutes stretch into hours
I lay in bed and watch
As the moon slowly creeps across the sky
And the stars dance in and out
I think of you
Broken promises
Spilled wine carpet stain
Dying fire, shattered dish
All seems familiar yet strange
The clock ticks loudly
Echoing in my brain
I turn over once more
To stare at the wall
No end in sight
Then morning once again

©2017
(from my book **It Is Still Morning**)

Chapter 3

When Dragons and Angles Collide
(Modern & Traditional Haiku & Senryu)
2017

colored ink illustration converted to B&W by Ann Christine
Tabaka, reduced in size

a time before time
dragons and angels collide
into a new earth

lazy summer day
bare feet giggle with delight
on cool moist grass

rainy day
the world reflected in
rippled puddles

early morning fog
blinks to greet another day
with half sleepy eyes

sketch by Ann Christine Tabaka, reduced in size

June dandelions
faeries dance on air
fulfilling wishes

dreams rush past
raging river swollen with
yesterday's rain

photo album
the past comes alive
time machine

mischievous night
moon pays peek-a-boo
on windowsill

windy summer day
swirling colors fill the air
kaleidoscope world

celestial event
magic lights up the night sky
meteor shower

Chapter 4

Everlasting
(A Lifetimeof Poems)
2017

pen & ink illustration by Ann Christine Tabaka, reduced in size

Dance of the Sanderlings

Little sanderlings
Playing tag
With the incoming tide
Feet ablur
While racing the waves
For tasty morsels
Buried in the wet sand
Bully gulls invade
Scattering the smaller birds
Circling around
They land once more
To continue their eternal waltz
With the ocean

©2017
(from my book **Everlasting**)

Afternoon Fun

Old movies
A celluloid circus
Of black and white and gray
Faded sepia tone
Slapstick and quirky
Romance and Noir
Dramatic and dark
Living life on the edge
I can almost hear the clicking
of the film reel as it spins
Rainy afternoon enjoyment
Popcorn in hand
Swaddled in an afghan
With cat in lap
A make-believe world feels real
For one afternoon

©2017
(from my book **Everlasting**)

Jigsaw

Life …
It is a puzzle
That we try to put together
Endlessly
We search through the pile
Of various shapes and colors
The events and circumstances of our lives
Trying to find the pieces that fit
Gingerly connecting them together
One by one
Trying over and over again
To make all the small fragments
Interlock into a whole
At times we try to force the bits
Of our life into place
That never works out well
And we must try again
Often we get to the end
And the box is empty
Yet, we are still missing that one piece
But eventually
There before us is a beautiful picture
That is us

©2017
(from my book **Everlasting**)

Ode to a Cat

Oh killer of paper balls
And tormentor of squirrels
Laying at my feet
You have warmed your way
Into my heart

Soft vibrations emanate
At the touch of a hand
A sound so intoxicating
To those who are enchanted
By your spell

Murderous claws and fangs
Bared and ready for attack
Against the invisible enemy
Lurking safely behind
The flower pot

Luminous jade eyes
Capture the imagination
For some you are a god
Others see you as
An omen of evil

Oh unpredictable imp
And lover of comfort
You are a delight to me
And those others
Whom you allow in

©2017
(from my book **Everlasting)**

Ode to the Moon

Oh hazy moon
Half hidden in the evening mist
Peeking from behind wisps of clouds
As you frolic among the stars

You have mystified man
Since time immemorial
You have been hailed as a god
By the ancients

You fill the imagination with wonder
More songs and poems
Have been written about you
Than of love itself

You have been the earth's companion
For ages beyond count
You have witnessed untold extinctions and wars
While you stood your silent guard

At night you light the way
For weary travelers and lovers alike
You rule the tides, then eclipsed by the world
You disappear into the shadows

Man has touched you
And left his footprints
Forever on your surface
And still your magic remains

©2017
(from my book **Everlasting**)

Don't Blink

Morning fog
Greets the new day
Slowly opening
Sleepy eyes
Blinking
It misses the sun
That has gone into hiding
Searching for lost days
Chasing the night
Into the stars

©2017
(from my book **Everlasting**)

colored ink illustration converted to B&W image by Ann
Christine Tabaka, reduced in size

Disorientation

The whistle of a distant train pierces the night.
Loneliness swallows the darkness.
Unspoken words consume the mind.
Strange thoughts invade reality as walls close in.
Time painfully creeps by until almost at a standstill.
Slowly strangling the will of its ability to resist.
A disoriented half dream world,
where corners of the imagination
shatter into vibrant fragments,
in the eternal plight of sleeplessness.

©2017
(from my book **Everlasting**)

* Nominated for the **2017 Pushcart Prize in Poetry**
 (by *Ariel Chart*)

He Can No Longer See

He can no longer see
he is blind
not the physical blindness
that comes from illness or age
but a blindness of spirit
blinded to the truth
blinded to all beauty
groping in the darkness
of his own personal disease
feeling his way through life
a life that is desiccated and crumbling
dying of his own want
a greed that is all encompassing
he once had eyes
but they are useless now
he gouged them out himself
years ago
now he wanders aimlessly
through the wasteland of the damned

©2017
(from my book **Everlasting**)

Broken Calm

Pitch black
foreboding night
distant rumbles
a sharp crash of thunder
the sky is split in two
by a white-hot bolt of lightning
mighty trees bow to the wind
awakening sleeping beasts
the hearts of men race
pounding in their ears
bones rattle
teeth gnash
horripilation
as all await the next imminent strike
KABOOM!

©2017
(from my book **Everlasting**)

Wash Me Clean

Rain wash down over me
and sing away my tears.
I walk alone on whispers,
fragile as faith confronted.

The tension reaching out,
with languid fingers of longing
grasping at my throat.
Conclusions never complying.

Prayers go unanswered
floating on a sea of doubt.
The litany of lust prevails
devouring the holy with the damned.

I beseech the ancient ones
to rescue my true self
and let the rain cleanse
my desires with its song.

©2017
(from my book **Everlasting**)

The Unlearning of Truth

I heard the yelling and the crying
I heard the singing and the praying
Outside on the streets
It was the spring of 1968
The entire country exploded with fear
We were trapped behind a human wall
National Guard and Police on every corner
You could feel the hate
And almost taste the terror
That permeated the atmosphere
It could no longer be contained

Another great man had been assassinated
Sparking the flames that followed
I was young and idealistic
I stood hand in hand with my brothers
We tried to change that one small corner
Of our world
The only thing separating us was
The color of our skin
And I was on the wrong side of the street

The earth has turned 18,000 times
And traveled around the sun forty-nine
Much has changed since then
But the fear that instills hatred in the hearts of many
Still remains trapped in that volatile time
An ancient hatred of the unknown
We have achieved unfathomable advancements
In the past fifty years
And yet, we still have not learned how to live
Together in peace

Chapter 5

The Sound of Dragonfly Wings
Modern English Haiku & Senryu
2018

pen & ink illustration by Ann Christine Tabaka, reduced in size

a summer meadow
stained glass windows catch the sun
dragonfly wings

billowy clouds
paint brushstrokes
across watercolor sky

abandoned sunhat
playing tag with
the evening tide

white hydrangea
waving pompoms
for the croquet game

flock of blackbirds
a winding highway
heading south

frog's lily pad
a forgotten flip-flop
on a quiet lake

a gray dawn
falling from the sky
like plucked feathers

in the mist
dreams sail off
as pirate ships

nightfall
velvet arms
caress the dusk

black cat
jade eyes
reveal ancient mysteries

tattered seams
the soft comfort of
old worn blue jeans

false promises
fruit baskets filled with
wax delicacies

jazz club
a slice of heaven
on a paper plate

lights dim
horn wails
smoke and whiskey filled room

Chapter 6

Reaching for Dawn
2018

pen & inkillustration by Ann Christine Tabaka, reduced in size

Reaching for Dawn

The shades of dawn
falling like colorful feathers
plucked from the sky.

Sorrow, a distant friend with
sodden shoulder and sturdy
pose, no longer needed.

In hand, a timetable of
misbegotten deeds, to be
dispersed to the four winds.

The song was sung long ago.
The echo still remains, of
voices faint and far off.

I do not know the words.

Climbing the mountain,
altitude unknown, oxygen
thin as a noon shadow.

The pinnacle appears.
Breathing in clouds,
focus begins to dim.

Past fading into future, as
the dawn now turns pure gold.
The summit is within reach.

©2018 (from my book **Reaching for Dawn**)

Laundry Day

Crisp white sheets bleached by the sun,
waving like so many flags, surrendering
to the turbulence of life. Memories of days
long past, when life seemed simpler, and
yet felt harder, all at the same time.

I can envision my mother standing there,
her graying hair pulled back, donning a
patchwork apron; carefully taking each
rolled up damp sheet from the basket
with her age worn hands, and shaking it
out to hang upon the rope line.

White sheets, symbolic of her surrender,
giving herself in to a life of drudgery and
poverty. Love's labors lost to past dreams
that never were. Blinded by the brightness
of the white, as she herself was bleached
and withered by the blistering sun. I still
feel her pain today, all these years later.

Certain images evoke strong memories,
taking us back in time. Like a daydream
coming into focus, I can almost touch
mymother in my mind's eye. Then,
reality snaps its finger, as the sheets
begin to wave their surrender once again.

©2018 (from my book **Reaching for Dawn**)

Beware of the Quiet

Do not allow the quietness
that saturates the halls of night
break through the dawn.

For it will shatter all perception
of time and space, grabbing
reality by the throat.

Then where will the sense
of priorities lie, except among
the fallow ruins of an ancient past,

defying the depth of disregarded
wisdoms, challenging all known facts,
until there is no truth left.

Adhere to the movement of slow
creeping convention, while the
lamented longings are just out of reach.
For the quiet is rooted deep within.

©2018 (from my book **Reaching for Dawn**)

And the Rains Came

The storm had passed, after raging for hours.
A deluge of major proportions. Last evening
the main road was a swift moving river. Now
it was up to the ankles in slimy brown mud.

Everyone scratched their heads. What was
to be done now? Even the dog from across
the way stood frozen with concern, like some
comical statue. He seemed determined that
muddy paws were not to be part of his day.
Mud baths being for swine, and not canine.

Shattered tree corpses caught up in the
flooding, their branches emerging from the
mud like a scorched forest. Reminiscent of
a bizarre miniature landscape from an old
science fiction film, barren and colorless.

Old folks tell of similar storms. They
happened decades ago, or so it is said,
memories being such as they are, stories
cannot be relied upon from their retelling.

Looking up, the sky hung heavy and
dark. More rain will come, adding to the
already distressing situation. Even the
birds are silent. No echoing songs from
the woodlands. The dead quiet, an omen.

We all walked away knowing more mud
was coming, and for the moment, nothing
could be done. And then once again,
the rains came as if there was no end.
And, perhaps, there wasn't.

©2018
(from my book **Reaching for Dawn**)

watercolor painting of "Daffodils"
converted to B&W image by Ann Christine Tabaka, reduced in
size

Eternal Game

Night sounds amble away with starlight
at their heels. Seeking out the yawn of
morning's sleepy outstretched arms.

Hours, four and twenty, play tag
amongst themselves. A game
the moon knows all too well.

Dreams come to rest on shoulders
white as milk, until the sunlight beckons,
with eyes the color of sapphires.

The story is perpetual beyond the span
of time. Eternally chasing its own tail
through the universe in pursuit
of a brilliant golden sun.

©2018
(from my book **Reaching for Dawn**)

Brokenness

There is no black and white
anymore. Everything is gray
as I wade through Indecision.

I do not remember how to pray.
My knees now fail to bend.
Desperate hands forget how to fold.

The words no longer form in
my effete heart, nor do they
pour forth from my mute mouth.

Emptiness reaching out, searching
beyond a sacred scripture, for a
faith larger than taught words.

Malignant desires, like invasive
vines, overtopping the forest,
choking out all natural beauty.

Frenetic lives cluttered with
belongings, void of any true value.
Broken beings in need of healing.

An urge to be filled. A question
to be answered. A new spiritual
awakening rising from within.
Broken no more.

©2018 (from my book **Reaching for Dawn**)

An Evening in September

Evening reaches across and blankets the land.
Tall stalks kissed pink by the glow of the setting sun.

Row after row of fence posts stand at attention.
A lone crow perched atop a rail surveys the expanse.

In the field a one-eyed scarecrow stares back menacingly.
Darkness falls earlier as the hours of daylight abate.

Soon harvest time will arrive with its thunderous
mechanical beasts looming over the landscape,
belching black smoke and churning up clouds of dust,
as they reap the golden crops.

As the harvesters cleave the shafts they will leave
the refuse in their wake like so many fallen soldiers.

The crow looks over the bounty of ripe grain,
aware that it will soon be time for him to go.
Flying to a place of safety far from the noisy
metal monsters that now sit on the horizon in wait.

The scarecrow smiles knowing he has done his job well.

©2018
(from my book **Reaching for Dawn**)

One More Ride

Father worked the rails. Free
passage was our rite. Hours
rocking back and forth to the
constant rhythm of the train.

Foreheads pressed to cool
fuliginous windows, scenery
streaming by at a giddying pace.
Large cities, small towns,
virescent farm land, all ablur.

The somnolent clickety-clack
of wheels motoring onward.
Miles of track laid north to
south, east to west. Once the
lifeblood of transportation.

Memories, hard and soft now
collide, as once great escapades
also blur in my aging mind. One
more ride, yes one more ride,
and I shall soon be home.

©2018
(from my book **Reaching for Dawn**)

Jazz Club

The lights dim
        a horn wails
smoke and whiskey   fill the room

A voice like silk
        from some long past era
hearts mellow
        tears spill

Bodies sway
        fingers snap
Feet   s h u f f l e
        across the floor

Hushed voice   conversations
        glasses clink
            toes tap

Drunk on
        atmosphere
a slice of heaven   on a paper plate

High notes - low bows
        the jazzman walks off
            claps and whistles follow
               the lights rise

©2018
(from my book **Reaching for Dawn**)

Beyond the Reach of Time

Black crow
      sings a song
unknown to man.
Forest awakes,
        answering back.

Vestiges of life
        fall from the sky
like winter snow.
Existence comes into being.

Dawn bursts forth,
        day enters.
Stars blink their goodbyes.
So it is said, so it is done.

The guardian steps forth
        as light emerges.
Time lapses …
Burgeoning worlds converge.

The sky is alive.
        I hear his song.
Black crow flies off,
Beyond the reach of time.

©2018
(from my book **Reaching for Dawn**)

A House in Ruin

Walking past the old dwelling,
looking in through doleful eyes.

She is an abandoned house,
tenebrous windows, crumbling

walls. Visions of the past haunt
her rooms, as she combs through

the disarray. A dark shadow
lurking in the closet evokes images

of some forgotten past. Peeling
paint, chipped plaster, her joints

are creaking hinges. Her mind,
a cobwebbed attic peppered with

incoherent words. She wades
through the rubble of her own

demise. A house that has stood
the storms of time. Age demands

its toll. Turning to walk away, the
once beloved house is left in ruin.

©2018
(from my book **Reaching for Dawn**

Chapter 7

Just Breathe
(A book of micro-poems)
2018

sketch by Ann Christine Tabaka

dragon's breath,
last breath,
breath of life
breathe already
do not hold your breath
your life depends on it

pen to paper
the feeling of
pure release
          - *poetry*

it is too much to bear
knowing you this way
I must sing to the birds
the trees understand

hold me in your arms
but do not touch me
I am ice
and I will melt

diamonds raining from trees
the sun on melting snow
                    – early March

there are times in our lives
that will remain with us forever
even when the mind no longer remembers
they have become part of us
woven into our very being
you are one of those times

the sun rises too slowly
and sets too fast
in the blink of an eye
the future is the past

destined to be
who I am
fact and fate collide

fingertip to lips
I ask the world for silence
    - *shhhh*

growing up I had two older brothers
wore boys' hand-me-downs
climbed trees and played soldiers
I was one of the guys
I never wanted to be a girl ...
until I met you

Chapter 8

No More Hallelujahs
2019

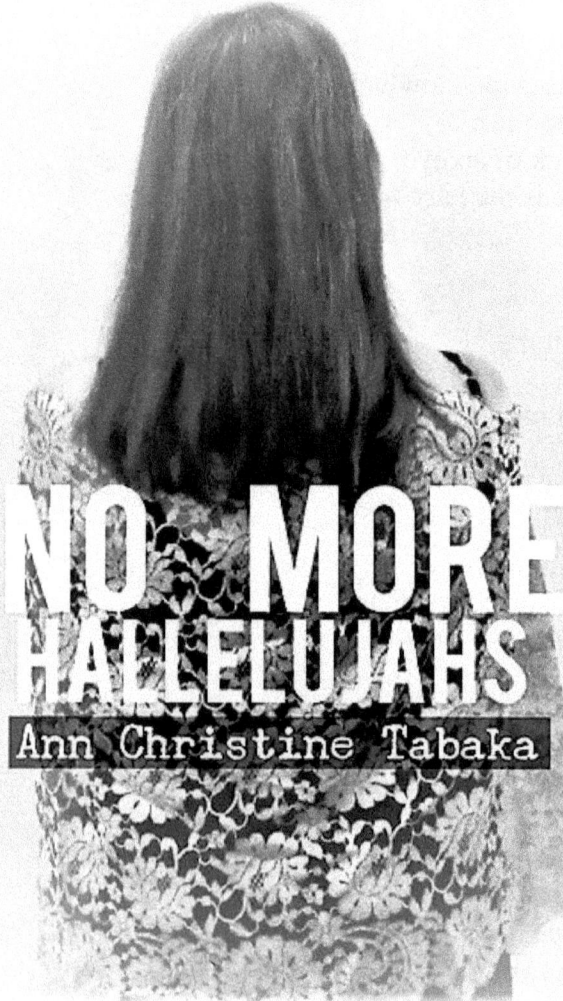

No More Hallelujahs

No more hallelujahs.
A withering chorus dies.
Words crumble into dust.

Paper thin whispers
weep for their loss.

Standing lonely on the side,
a voice cries out for redemption.

Single steps and double jumps
across a nonexistent page.

Invisible to all but a few
who seek the immortality of the moment.

Too long have the carols
not been sung,
not been performed,
not been heard.

Hallelujahs ring out no more.

©2019
(from my book **No More Hallelujahs**)

Little White Lies

Unforeseen circumstances
of [nebulous] actions,
drive deep into the
foretelling of consequence.
Carried on the back of
hate's [wagging] tongue
are lies that fear to be exposed.
Of gratitude and grandeur
a story is told,
not believing a word of itself.
Counting countenance and
eyeing [damned] effluence,
it continuously crawls
from its chamber of cataclysm.
Condemning a nature of incredulity,
maintaining only in its [own] truth.
Lusting for embodiment of soul,
it sequesters the veracity of all.

©2019
(from my book **No More Hallelujahs**)

The Inconsistencies of Life

Inconsistency rests
on weary shoulders
abducted by fame's
glittery prize.

Not knowing a word of worth
when held out before its eyes.

A pentad of pendulums
swing just out of reach,
a sweeping arch
from right to wrong.

From virtue to ruination,
never stopping long enough
to perceive equilibrium.

Indecisive lives
grasp at lustful desires,
never satisfied
with what is at hand.

The constant of being inconstant,
fickle, faithless, and false,
a tiring act of seeking
what cannot be found.

©2019
(from my book **No More Hallelujahs**)

I Remember Her

I remember her
standing there,
outstretched arms of love.
Taking in all our sins,
she paid the penance,
saying her Hail Marys.
Forgiving all forgiveness,
in her martyr way.
Her quiet strength
filled the room.
Keeping all pain to herself,
no one knew she was there.
Present, yet unperceivable
was her whispered prayer.
She held no malice,
spoke no hate,
though tortured was her lot.
She faded from existence
just as she arrived,
alone and unnoticed,
by all but me.
I remember her
standing there,
outstretched arms of love.

©20219
(from my book **No More Hallelujahs**)

Now I Lay me Down to Sleep

Now I lay me down to sleep,
sky burning alcohol red.
Crimson flames consume
my breath as the air ignites.
Death has come for me at last,
he stands outside my door.
Prayers pour forth from
a mouth of sand, Contents
for I cannot speak a word.
I whimper in fear, I try to cry out.
There is no redemption left.
It is time to lay to rest
and sleep the eternal sleep.

©2019
(from my book **No More Hallelujahs**)

Price of a Coin

A turnstile coin
falls in slow motion,
hits with a rattle and a clink.
Rolling to a stop at his feet.
I bend to pick it up,
retrieving long lost visions
of a love that used to be.
Turning from the past,
I walk away.
A burning ache
pulls at me,
filling my heart with sorrow.
I look back one last time.
Coin pocketed,
I board the train
to my redemption.

©2019
(from my book **No More Hallelujahs**)

Chapter 9

Words Spill Out
2019

Words Spill Out

Torn open,
words spill from my wound,
leaping off the paper,
cascading to the floor.
Chasing them,
they tumble out the door.
Reaching out, they elude my grasp.
Following I become lost.

An empty ache torments my mind,
wondering where they vanished to.
Capturing one,
then another,
but there is no cohesion.
Phrases running amok in my head,
drift slowly to my pen.

But alas, there is no tale to tell,
only words stacked up one
against another.
They will not align themselves
to paint the image that I hold within.
No panacea for my plight.
Another day,
another week,
and words spill out again.

©2019
(from my book **Words Spill Out**)

A Song to the Twilight

Ruby studded sky,
the horizon calls to me.
It knows my name by heart.
I have stood here all eternity,
watching a coral glow of evening,
as geese fly past the moon.
Stories of past lives
unfold before my eyes.
On wings of imagination
my mind takes flight.
The night is my master.
The night is my friend.
It folds me in its warm embrace,
darkness pulls me in,
like a lover waiting to be kissed.
I sing a song to the twilight
with voice soft and sweet.
Dancing stars join the refrain.
Night is my salvation,
its magic lives within.
Everlasting is its song
from beginning to the end.

©2019
(from my book **Words Spill Out**)

Silent no More

The silence of a thousand years
is broken with a whisper,
emanating from
the heartbeat of oppression.

Time can no longer restrain truth.
It breaks open sins of the past.
Soaring above the rabble,
chains fall off,
secrets bleed out.

Blackened bones of our ancestors
crumble in desperation.
It is my turn to speak.
My words are winter rain.

Bare limbs reaching from the pyre,
their cries can no longer
be buried alive with their bodies.

Blue songs and green desires
melt away in an inferno.
Annealed, weak become strong.

Pained voices unite,
shedding off their shroud,
never more to be silenced.

©2019
(from my book **Words Spill Out**)

Face like Vodka

A face like vodka,
a soul like wine,
cocktail of life
drained dry by time

Your cruel departure
left a hole in the universe.
All existence has ceased.

Drowning in intoxicants,
vestiges of sanity gone,
a scent of grapes lingers on.

Birds overhead observe me
grounded supine,
my roots reaching downward
Into the dead earth.

Searching for a reason to exist,
dreams like bourbon,
voice like rum.

You are gone forever.
Now life becomes a river
of drunken deception.

©2019
(from my book **Words Spill Out**)

Smoke and Mirrors

Words that do not say a thing,
spout vague persuasions,

dancing around on a tongue of fire.
Heads tilting, nodding, turning.

What was that you said?
Writing a thesis of the damned,

we follow bread crumbs of doubt.
Ring around the Rosie, time has

all but passed. Sweet garlands
of discovery, upon the ocean cast.

A breath held blue, a quandary spent,
we plunge ahead anew.

Devoid of sense, we seek the prize,
a lanced boil. Meanwhile paintings

of colorful descent adorn a contrived
world. Rising from the throng,

visions of disbelief profess to be real.
Fabricated phrases fill our lives

with words that say but nil.
Alas, all is smoke and mirrors,
… and smoke

©2019
(from my book **Words Spill Out**)

Dust to Dust

Apple pie mornings,
childhood scraped knee,
take me away again.

Words spoken in secret
to ears that won't hear
rattle around in the wind.

Once upon a times
don't exist anymore,
the universe swallowed them whole.

Hand held friendships
hopscotch off,
chalk washed clean by tears.

Distant moves,
letters few, then none.
Woeful news arrives.

Missed laughter,
tucked beneath the earth.
Another venerable sidekick
dances with the dust.

©2019
(from my book **Words Spill Out**)

Dry Spell

Fissured mud,
dry, hard, gray.
So many interlacing
fingers reaching out
in every direction,
crumble to the touch.

Arid summer,
sucking the breath from life.
Languishing thirst.
Wilted flora bow their heads.
Fallen warriors lack resilience
to withstand the furnace blast.

Parched earth,
crying out for sustenance.
No clouds in sight.
Not a drop of compassion
to be found.

Cruel season of drought,
unexpected curse.
Farmers pass their hats
and lay low,
hands folded in prayer.

Rotted fruit.
Tiny shriveled globes of despair.
Shrunken heads
hang limp and forlorn
upon dying hosts.

Time stands still.
Torrid air strangles all
within its grasp.
I exhale the dragon
from my lungs.

Scorched clay drifts from my hand,
dispersed into the atmosphere.
Well of hope, dry as dust.
Foreign to some years,
a vengeance in others.

All promise lost,
walking away
Then …
faces turn upward
in disbelief,
as forgiveness rains from the sky

©2019
(from my book **Words Spill Out**)

Darkness Unfolds

It's Friday night.
The wolves have devoured their
portion. Now it's time for the
scavengers to come out and feed.

Ignoring a distant storm,
eyes close, ears shut. Pain
forgotten, but not erased.

Beyond all comprehension
night breaks through the
dawn, with only so much
salvation to go around.

The smallness of our lives,
filled with such desires and
greed. Yearning for
Friday night once again.

©2019
(from my book **Words Spill Out**)

Street Corner

Alligator skin and button eyes.
The devil himself would cry
at seeing such a man.
Twisted hand held out in despair,
begging for a pittance.
Gaping wound of hunger
weeps out injustice spent for a dime.
Cardboard castle and newspaper
bed against a bitter cold blast of truth.
Breath held tight in defiance to a
storm of unrepented sins.
Again, and yet again I say,
but for the grace ….
Time turning orange to brown,
fingers aching blue.
Discarded man, hunched figure,
a pile of rags upon the sidewalk.
Head bowed low, not in contrition.
Empty shell with hollow stare.
Words of ice melted by the fire
of unforgiving masses.
No one sees, no one cares.
A procession of woe slowly
spirals ever downward into
a whirlpool of the damned.
Tear-stained vision of
impassioned pain, forever cursed
to walk this earth alone,
calling street corner home.
But for the grace …

©2019
(from my book **Words Spill Out**)

It Is Cold

It's cold old man.
"Yes, I remember cold."
Put on your coat old man.
"Yes, I used to have a coat.
it was green, such a lovely shade of green."
Here is your coat, it is brown.
"No, not my coat.
My coat is green, like the color of her eyes."
Whose eyes?
"My darling wife. Where is she?
I have been waiting for her all day."
Your wife is no longer with us.
"Where did she go?
She told me she would be here."
Maybe she is outside.
We should go look.
Put on your coat, it is cold old man.
"Yes, I remember cold."

©2019
(from my book **Words Spill Out**)

Chapter 10

Keep Breathing
(A book of micro-poems)
2020

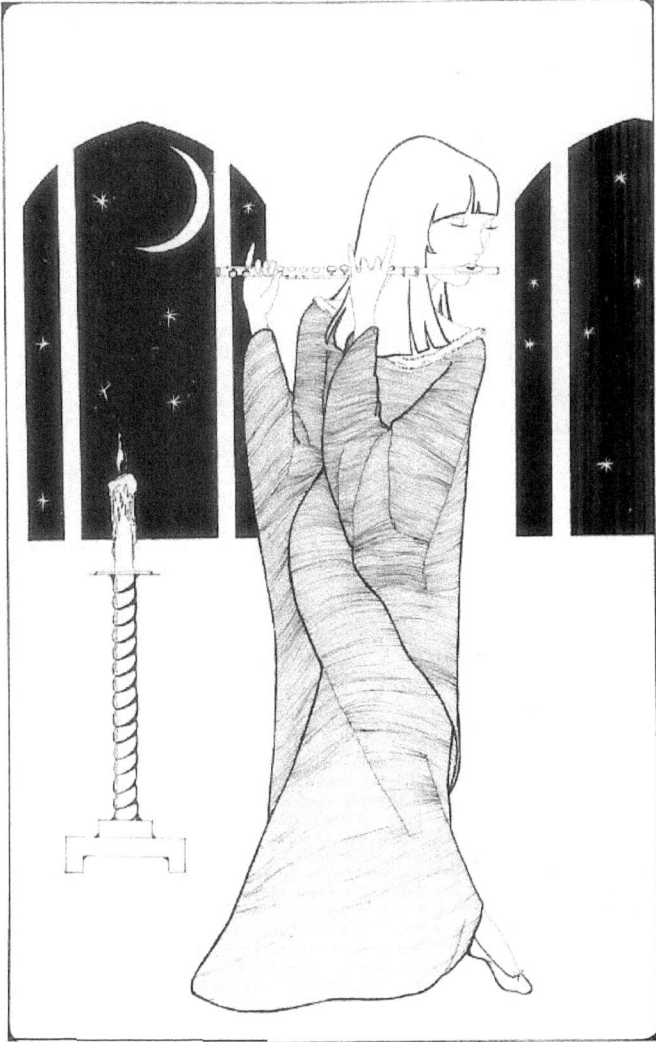

pen & ink illustration by Ann Christine Tabaka, reduced in size

loving you
is the hardest thing
I've ever done
- *sacrifice*

we strive for perfection
only to fail
while ignoring
the attainable goal
within our reach

the boisterous rumbling of a kitten
all too soon becomes
the muted purr of old age

I walked inside
your love
like a child
into a candy store

growing up
we did not speak of such things
we turned our heads
and hid our eyes
the innocence of childhood
washed away
with a single tear

I walked inside
your love
like a child
into a candy store

a hole in one sock
a lonely mate
joins the mismatched pile
hoping for new life

we tried too hard
fire and ice
we repelled each other

allow yourself
to fall apart
and
come back together
when you are ready
– *grieving*

if I hang upside-down
from this tree
long enough
I shall become
a child again

Chapter 11

Running Backwards in Time
2020

Deep Within

I remember a place deep inside,
that used to hold love dear.

Treasures buried within
the confines of my heart.

Speak to me my son,
tell me where the years have gone.

For time has stolen youth from me,
and now you are a man.

Gone are the moments of childhood joy,
when you used to take my hand.

Lost among stray memories
of bed time stories and fairy tales.

We cannot go back to golden days
of playing in the sun.

Yet, old age cannot take you from me,
not now or ever more.

In my heart and in my mind,
you are forever my little boy.

©2020
(from my book **Running Backwards in Time**)

His Daughter

He left behind his curse,
it followed him to the end.
Blood cannot be divided,
cannot be distilled.
I am my father's daughter.

Coal black eyes stare back,
a violent storm that would not die.
Time does not forget
a hand raised against the past.

We hid from each other's sins.
There were not enough tears
to make things work,
nor to make amends.

You were your father,
who I never knew.
I became you,
as did my son.

No one understands
how blood carries memory,
and thus bonds our fate.
The curse lives in me.
I am my father's daughter.

©2020
(from my book **Running Backwards in Time**)

100

Meteor Shower

A wish flashes across the sky,
trailed by blinding glory.
Eyes closed, breaths held,
it vanishes in a blink.

Hearts race across the moon
in buoyant anticipation.
Hope beyond hope
a granting of desire.

A flicker of childhood
held in ancient folklore,
unlocking forgotten joy.
A single blaze of light.

Believing, not believing,
we never abandon
the wonder in a moment,
wishing on a star.

©2020
(from my book **Running Backwards in Time**)

A Story Lives Within Us All

There were other stories,
ones that no one told.
They lurked behind closed doors,
hiding in sheltered whispers.

Rumors of broken lives,
that once lived among the ruins.
A surgical analysis
of a situation - exposed truth.

A wounded heart stands alone,
seeking its repentance.
Never knowing fault is not
of its own making.

Beyond any barriers
of fallen existence,
we fight for our beliefs.
They define who we are.

A story held - a story told.
A story lives within us all.
Cloaked, hidden from the world,
itmaturates in its own misery.

©2020
(from my book **Running Backwards in Time**)

Life Melting

Life melting,
like snow in spring.
Dripping down,
one dream at a time.
Slipping through our fingers.
Seeping between crevices
where no light shines,
beyond the reach of promise.
Prisms of winged desire,
falling in slow motion.
Forming small rivulets
that grow with every breath.
As life flows rapidly downstream,
wisps of imagination,
evaporate in the sun.
The beauty of a dying season,
giving birth to the next.

©2020
(from my book **Running Backwards in Time**)

Garment of Pain

Trying to forget
pain sewn into
the hem of my life,
with stitches
straight and precise.
No scissor
can cut me free.
Adamantine thread of dolor,
pulled tight,
knotted and
tucked deftly.
Perfect garment of malaise,
worn without
a thought of redemption.
Cold truth filtrates
through loose woven cloth.
Frayed edges
hold a nebulous reality,
that pain cannot escape.

©2020
(from my book **Running Backwards in Time**)

Not of this World

And the crescent moon a cradle
where I wrap my sleep in dreams,

that wander beyond galaxies
to places I have seen.

To dip my toes in stardust,
and walk among gods of ancient myth,

while searching for the meaning of love
that does not exist.

And I wake upon a shoreline
of a distant far-off land,

where nightingales rouse the morning,
with crystal notes of joy.

To be gathered all together
in a world of lost and found,

never to be returned to
a life that is earth bound,

For I am not of this world.

©2020
(from my book **Running Backwards in Time**)

Hiding in Plain Sight

Long lost treasures
and mismatched pieces
filling lonely days.
Each item holds a memory
to occupy my mind,
sifting through a maze
of forgotten artifacts.

A map to nowhere,
a key that does not fit,
tangled ribbons dance
with rubber bands.
Odd screws and old receipts,
all join in a mix of dreams
and once clever ideas.

A long searched for pen
hides just out of reach.
Upon further observation,
notions blend with objects
in a chaotic composition.
Beautiful clutter fills
my junk drawer of reality.

(from my book **Running Backwards in Time**)

Whispered Tones

Do not speak to me
in whispered tones.
I wish to hear a clear
loud ringing of the bell.
No hushed words
to hide a truth that does not exist.
The past does not preside,
except in one's own mind.
We hide so well within ourselves,
gambling trusted memories.
Circumstances do not allow
the reliving of lost lives.
I want to shout to the mountains.
I want to sing to the seas.
A conversation that opens up
the wounds of all who bleed.
It is time to confront the beast.
It is time to tell the story.
We can no longer conceal,
what we cannot convey.
Do not speak to me
in whispered tones.
Veracity is at hand.

©2020
(from my book **Running Backwards in Time**)

Snow Day

Taste now
the different colors
of the sun,
filtered through
brisk winter air.

Delicious dreams
float overhead
just out of reach,
while crystalline hope
clings to trees.

A world of white
sparkling blindness
encasing all,
on a bed of fresh
bleached sheets.

Growing younger
with anticipation,
the child emerges
and takes flight,
on the first snow day.

©2020
(from my book **Running Backwards in Time**)

Wonderland

I sing a song beyond the sea
where feathers float on dreams
and cactus flowers bloom.
Where lazy afternoon hours
sneak glimpses at sunset.
Where time has no meaning
for it counts itself in breaths,
and clouds of many colors
drift just out of reach.
Where laughter fills the morning light
reflected off the dew,
and nighttime touches dusk,
to soothe a weary soul.
I walk among wishes
held deep within a sigh.
Where ferns cast lacy shadows
upon sparkling rippled lakes,
and enchantment rules the dawn.
I sing a song beyond the sea.
My song is heard and answered,
carried on an eagle's cry.

©2020
(from my book **Running Backwards in Time**)

My Little Gypsy

Fiery jade eyes pierced the night,
leading me to you.

Seeking shelter from the wild,
abandoned as you were.

Hungry for food and touch,
you were an easy catch.

A tiny fluff of gray and peach,
a tortoiseshell beauty.

Never had I seen
a face as sweet as yours.

Ball of playful purrs,
and mouser supreme,

you filled my life with love
for close to eighteen years.

Now a small satin box
holds the remains of my heart.

How can I live without you,
my little Gypsy Cat?

©2020
(from my book **Running Backwards in Time**)

Chapter 12

And Still I Had These Dreams
2020

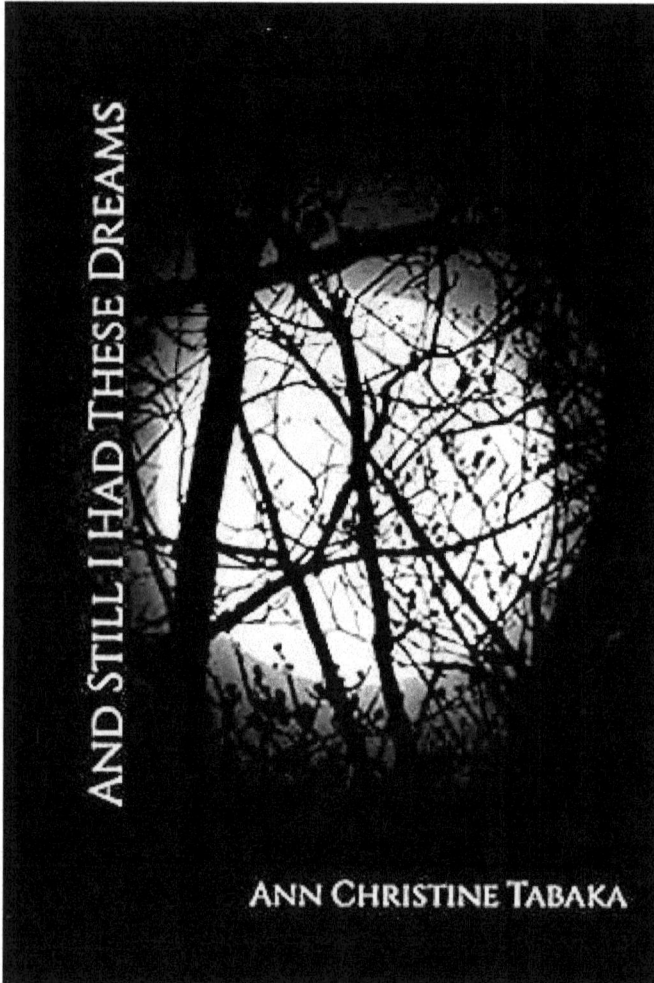

My Garden

It is easy to forget you,
the way you stand there
looking lost among the daisies.
Blossoms sprouting from every pore.
Your black eyes, now as empty seeds.
You never really tried to grow
outside the trellised wall.
You clung like some lost vision of
green lizards and snakes.
But who am I to blame,
when blaming is on call?
I knew better than to
plant you deep within my heart.
Now as autumn is at hand
and butterflies take wing,
your dying petals disperse
to the four winds.

©2020
(from my book **And Still I Had These Dreams**)

Summer's Fallen Memories

The peach trees were in bloom again.
Sweetness dripping like love's first kiss.

Sunlit eyes smiled past the dawn,
as we walked on summer's path.

Times past were strewn upon
a ground of overripe memories.

A longing well past its prime.
We knew better then,
but did not heed the raven's warning.

White to pink to brown,
we discolor and shrivel to dust.

Winged hope flies overhead out of reach,
as peach blossom petals snow softly to earth.

©2020
(from my book **And Still I Had These Dreams**)

The Beast Shall Have its Way

Speak not to me of distant times,
the candle has grown dim.
Tired days of illusion wander
past a forgotten yesterday.

A beast breathes down my neck
as life stares me in my visage.
Too many questions
have walked this way before.

The desert does not give up her secrets
buried in the dancing sands.
There is no escaping circumstance
once etched upon the cliffs.

We have but a moment left
to relive the life we lost.
We are wild animals,
we cannot be tamed.
The beast shall have its way.

©2020
(from my book **And Still I Had These Dreams**)

First Step: Transformation

The child walked away,
he did not look back.
Trees were his only witness.

A lifetime of hidden shame,
sins of the father,
no longer a shadow clinging to his flesh.

The forest swallowed him whole,
and there he remains,
breathing in new life.

Shedding his scales,
he grew branches
thriving among the greenwood.

©2020
(from my book **And Still I Had These Dreams**)

The Edge of Time

And if I stand on the edge of time watching,
will the seeker find me there tomorrow?

Clouds drift beneath emerald peaks,
blocking out humanity.

Shall I witness the righting of all wrongs,
as the sun burns through the fog?
I await the coming of truth.

For I do not exist anymore,
I am just an apparition of my fantasy,
floating through time and space.

Can tomorrow be a reality,
if it does not exist today?

Atop the pinnacle of imagined thought,
we reach for that which we cannot see.

All the while trying to understand
what beyond our crystal eyes,
vanishes in a wink.

So I stand and ponder thusly,
as wind carries me over the edge,
and the seeker takes my hand to guide.

©2020
(from my book **And Still I Had These Dreams**)

A Popcorn Afternoon

My toes are cold,
as I sit watching old Black & White movies on TV.
The popcorn is salty, and my mind wanders off
to yardwork that needs to be tended to.
The day is too long, but never long enough,
for the solitary life that swallows me up.
Shall I go get my slippers, or sit here and suffer?
So many mundane items to check off my list.
A list written in blood on a rain smudged window,
that never is open to the fresh air.
Dozing off, popcorn spills, scattering on the floor.
Startled, the cat runs off to hide.
Time to get up, to find where I am, who I am,
as my cold bare toes hit the floor,
crushing kernels of salty popcorn underneath.

©2020
(from my book **And Still I Had These Dreams**)

Reality Sets in

On the outer edge of reality,
I planted my dreams.
What seed should I sow,
to resurrect the image
of what I want to be?
Salt air and harsh winds
have corroded me.
My hands no longer
weave the silken thread.
I fought to the end,
but lost the beginning,
when you were by my side.
Soft words and hard kissesvanished
with thearid soil of despair.
Logic refuses to move forward.
So, off I walk,
poppy seeds in hand,
colorful dreams tripping off my palm.
I see the edge become clear.

©2020
(from my book **And Still I Had These Dreams**)

A Thousand Light Years Away

Distant stars, held in our hands,
a thousand light years past.
Seeking a reason for existence,
our disguise falls away.
Plummeting down a black hole
into infinity, abstract notions rise.
Finding oneself in a vision of doubt,
a corner is turned.
Never knowing, always guessing,
the substance of one's path.
The plurality of truth
lends a guiding light.
There are no answers beyond
what or why, nothing to ascertain.
Firmaments collapsing within our grasps.
Stars are born, and stars die,
while bewilderment takes hold.
We are but children of the sky,
reaching for the future,
with distant stars within our hands.

©2020
(from my book **And Still I Had These Dreams**)

My Brother's Keeper

You sit on the roof at night asking questions,
trying to solve mysteries of the universe.
But my brain doesn't work like that.
I watch you with rapt curiosity while shaking my head.
The heavens sing you a song I cannot hear,
it is only for you.
Staring deeply into the dark void,
you know things no one else will ever understand.
You build a picket fence
around the moon with your mind,
and arrange the planets in your garden,
burying them deep in a primordial soup.
$e = mc^2$ is etched upon your soul.
Savant or saint, I know not which,
but you see truths beyond the ages.
I am too afraid to reach out and touch you
for fear that some strange energy
will render me immobile.
I cannot save myself.
I cannot save you.
The chill of the winter night fills your lungs
and exhales a dream.
Frozen mist forms a halo around your raven hair.
What is it that you seek?
You in your solitary wonderment,
not letting anyone else in,
not even me.

©2020
(from my book **And Still I Had These Dreams**)

And Still I Had These Dreams

And still, I had these dreams.
Dreams of grandeur, iced in white frosting.
Waking to the truth.
A truth that no longer resides
beside the waterfall of hope.
Reaching for conclusions,
my eyes do not open fully.
Yawning my farewell
to all the glittery trinkets
set forth before the illusion.
A time so long ago,
that memories fail to adhere.
Buried alive in anticipation,
of a tomorrow that will not be.
Sweet songs of triumph
written in the icing,
now melting from neglect.
The night, no longer young,
as I am not.
We join hands in celebration,
the letting go of false intent.
Closed eyes to deep breath,
I succumb to a reality set before me.
And still, I had these dreams.

©2020
(from my book **And Still I Had These Dreams**)

Chapter 13

Pondering the Shoreline of Existence
2020

pen & ink illustration by Ann Christine Tabaka, reduced in size

October Night

Walking barefoot on wet sand,
counting stars.
Heartbeat synced to rhythmic waves.
Thoughts reach out beyond galaxies.
I have been dismantled.
I am no longer whole,
parts of me strewn across a vast universe.
Existence reaches the vanishing point,
and all things become one.
Stopping to smell salt air,
sweater pulled close against cold wind.
A gull's cry brings me back to earth,
as waves wash over bare feet.

©2020
(from my book **Pondering the Shoreline of Existence**)

Swimming Upstream

I cannot swim away upstream
with you about my neck.
Some poor lost soul from
a time long before we met.
We are not who we were,
and yet we are who we are.
The weight of disintegrating
dreams, pulling us both down.

The albatross of lore
is here upon my chest,
caged within my ribs.
No battering-ram can set it free.
It has become part of me,
woven into the texture
of my own flesh.
Ripped from my womb,
an apparition, not of my own making.

I wade in knee-deep despair,
searching for absolution.
I sink deeper into the tears
cried out by all mankind.
My baptism is complete.
I am released from false hope,
accepting my penance,
forever swimming upstream.

©2020
(from my book **Pondering the Shoreline of Existence**)

Words in the Sand

I write my story upon sand.
Wind carries swirling words,
to distant thought.
Eroding sins/loss/loneliness.

Aeolian process shaping life.
Sun baked paragraphs
crumble amid camel footsteps.
Invading army of doubt ridden fear.

Cracked lips bleed, singing no more.
Once fertile shores, now arid dreams.
Sinking caverns, lost in time,
swallow my petitions.

Transgressions lead the way.
I pencil in the next chapter.
Is there room for more -
The desert is vast.

It is the nineteenth of forever.
Sands bury my soul.
I shall not be unearthed,
like some ancient scroll.
For I live in the swirling sands of time.

©2020
(from my book **Pondering the Shoreline of Existence**)

It Was Wednesday

It was Wednesday.
Winds were calm.
Sun peeked through branches
as it climbed the sky.

Windows open to sweet air
and bird songs.
Promises were made.
New life emerged from soft earth.

It was Thursday.
Darkness covered all.
Sad sighs emerged from within.
Everything was upside down.

Doors locked to fear.
Prayers flowed.
Hearts sought solace.
How quickly everything changed.

It was Friday,
Saturday,
then Sunday …
A little bird landed on my feeder.
Flowers opened to face the sun.

A glimmer of hope shone.
And people walked outside once more.

©2020
(from my book **Pondering the Shoreline of Existence**)

It Fell from the Sky

It fell from the sky
in a blue-green cast,
singing songs of the mundane.
Swept under the rug of indifference,
it continued to play its requiem.
It grew stronger
with each coarse breath it took.
Scratching the eyes out from
all who dare peer into its black soul.
The mountain rose before it
as the preacher raised his hands,
standing high upon the citadel.
We froze in fear.
He stood on stilts
reaching for the flight of birds,
while blossoms rained from trees.
Face to face the battle bled,
for it was a mighty foe.
Calling forth powers
only true evil can wield,
it towered above our holy mountain.
Moon ate the shadows.
Darkness ate the moon.
Sky began to fall.
Covered in broken stardust,
crushed beneath its weight,
the Sky Pilot sang his song of praise.
The mountain raised up higher
to circle with soaring birds.
All humanity joined hands.
Falling to its knees,
it fled this mortal realm,
returning to sky.

As ages passed,
a story told to this day
of the unnamed beast,
and how it fell from the sky.
A warning to all mankind.

(from my book **Pondering the Shoreline of Existence**)

A Father Who Never Was

Born of war and hunger -
        a stolen youth
                ripped from earth.

Lost within a vanquished spring
        as winter counted days.

Black eyes   -   a raven's call
follow what cannot be seen,
        vagrant visions, dark to light.

Tortured flesh, his inheritance
        passed on to each of us in turn.

A buried past   -   sunken deep,
                the depths of which
                        are unknown.

We played with death
as little toy soldiers marched.

In fear
we hid ourselves from him.

Asking for more than he could give,
a pathway to the sun.

His childhood   our childhood,
repeating the mantra
        never love.

Not knowing how to be a father, husband, son, brother …
he only knew how to die.

He was war and hunger,
writing his own epilogue.

©2020
(from my book **Pondering the Shoreline of Existence**)

My father and me, 1951

131

The Importance of a Daughter

She always wanted a girl –
       two boys later … I appeared.

The man could not be a father,
so, she raised us, worked, provided on her own.
       Sadness was our family name!

Years between siblings parted any bonds.
       My brothers left before I was aware.

Time passed / I began to understand -
       the importance of a daughter,
           as we traded places.

I never had a daughter –
at an early age
       a son was ripped from my mold
           in the early morning hours - a lost wailing
    soul.

Circumstance did not allow more children.
I was not prepared for such a role.   One would be my lot.
       One would be enough.

Regret flies on the wings of time.
Although, now in old age -
       sometimes, I miss what I did not have –
           the silken ties of mother to daughter.

©2020
(from my book **Pondering the Shoreline of Existence**)

Diurnal Succession

The shallow breath of evening,
as it settles in for night
       - weary from a long day of labors.

Seeking solace that goes beyond
       the waywardness of thought.

A bramble of faint images
       dissolve into dusk.

Night takes evening by the hand
       leading her home.

Red streaked night sky - fades into black.

Morning into evening,
as night steps off the edge,
       falling into a brilliant
            sunlit morning once again.

(from my book **Pondering the Shoreline of Existence**)

A Weed Among Roses

I am but a weed, amongst roses – despised by fragrant
petals, and those who cherish order   and   calm.

For I am chaos demanding to be uprooted.
    Thrown into the fire of hate   and   fear.

I am different than you, and you tremble.
You quake at my existence, for I am too near to you.
        You are more like me than you can admit.
A fact that appalls you.

More different than a million moons – shining down on a
dark night.

I lost my way long before you were born, or ever thought
into being.
    Time stretches out its lonely arms to grab you,
        and disseminate your thoughts among the thorns.

Once we were whole   and we wrapped ourselves into
distant galaxies, searching for stars to ride the wave home.

Seeds falling into reality, the garden grows   and
flourishes.
    Yet, weeds enter in, and ideals lose their way.
You cannot run from me   I am part of you.

You may be a rose, but you emerged from my womb.
    One cannot be without the other -
the distance is too great, and we are too small, too close,
too alike.
    We share the same pain.

(from my book **Pondering the Shoreline of Existence**)

134

Pondering the Shoreline of Existence

I was cleaned today.
I was put away / high upon a shelf,
  safely out of sight.
Left to macerate like some specimen in a jar.
Emotions raw – from entanglement.
Knife separates flesh from desire / sinew from pain.
Devoid of contrition - my penance is great.
Parmenides walked an ancient shoreline
pondering existence.
The sand beneath my feet is real,
yet it flows freely from my hand – back into the sea.
Dispersed throughout vast oceans,
  its identity is lost.
I am trapped in a world of my own sins.
If existence is freedom,
  then do I cease to exist?

©2020
(from my book**Pondering the Shoreline of Existence**)

Chapter 14

I No Longer Her You Sing
2020

watercolor painting of "Irises"
converted to B&W image by Ann Christine Tabaka, reduced in
size

I No Longer Hear You Sing, Mother of Mine

Today is a day like no other - bonds shatter into dust.
I lost you to the sheering wind - ashes loft on high.

You no longer sing out of tune to me,
evoking memories of tear-stained rain.

A fractured bird that cannot trill
has become my destiny.

Left alone among the masses - searching for a sign.
I will never be whole again.

It happened so long ago - or was it yesterday?
Remorseful - time got in the way.

We were flesh before we tore.
The womb calls us to rejoin.

©2020
(from my book **I No Longer Hear You Sing**)

Rain will Never be my Friend Again

I cannot see - I cannot feel.
The rain has blinded me - paralyzed me with its chill.

There was a time when rain was my playmate,
        my companion;
when it frolicked and splashed in my youth.

It washed away my tears - and refreshed my fatigue.
Now it depletes me of all joy.

It reminds me of the day you left.
The rain fell so hard that day.

Sorry, is all the doctor said,
        as the sheet became your shroud.

The rain never stopped.
The angels cried - lowering you into the earth.

The covering of umbrellas dispersed,
but I remained – unsheltered,
        slowly dissolving in the downpour.

Water holds memories, it is told.
        It will not let go.

Rain may dilute my tears,
but rain will never be my friend again.

©2020
(from my book **I No Longer Hear You Sing**)

The Heart of Winter

December shedher wings and flew away
giving room for January to grow anew
sunlight shimmers in frosty air
crystals sparkle from every branch
ice laced winter morn
pristine snow covers all
time is frozen - in a whisper
enchanting beauty of a harsh season
slowly waiting for spring thaw

©2020
(from my book **I No Longer Hear You Sing**)

A Trail That Leads Back Home

At the end of the field, at the edge of the woods,
is a trail that leads back home.
I speak to the forest, the trees reply.
They lift their heads, responding to my call.
Shrill bark of a red fox, shrieking like a lost child,
searching to find its way.
Yearning for its clan, sounds pierce the dark,
reverberating, penetrating a silent night.
I recognize myself in him, wandering alone,
seeking penance. But I am not as fearless as he.
He is my lost son, whom I have abandoned to the
trial of ages. For I could not keep him forever young.
I have no spells to cast that will stop the years.
I grow older, as does he.
So, I go to the place where he was conceived,
to make the forest my final abode.
I follow the trail that will lead me back to him.
There, I lie down on a bed of fern and dry leaves.

©2020
(from my book **I No Longer Hear You Sing**)

Talking to My Younger Self

Heed well;
for my words are but a concept in your young mind.
We cannot pass through the barrier of time. I am

a memory that you do not know. Looking back
many years, we traveled seventy journeys around

this sun; seventy-one, counting heartbeats within our
mother's womb. Remembering all the tears shed; all

the mountains scaled; all the sins buried deep.
I tell you, do not look back, do not fear the future,

do not give up hope. Your passion and your desires
are held in a secret trove; hidden from all but you

and me. They are not to be revealed to a hungry world,
ingesting each weary breath. Past-lives tumbling off the

edge of an eyeblink. It is too late for regrets. It is never
too late to change. We have shared a history that no

one else can share. We touched the sky, we sailed through
clouds. Icy oceans held us up, as we were about to sink.

We loved, we lost, we survived this far. We do not see
where we are going, but we know where we have been.

Listen, yes listen to the voice within. Your future is my
past.

©2020
(from my book **I No Longer Hear You Sing**)

In Life, there is Always an Endgame

The TV blares.   Stars fall.   Matches spark.
Another day has spent.

Minutes reach for hours, and time forgets its name.

I am passed who I am.
I do not know the way.

A bed calls out from nowhere.
     Blankets tumble to the floor.
Restless memories
   wrapped in silk,
     tear apart.

He never comes home anymore.   I never ask why.

Shadows dance on walls.
   Dissolution is in the wind.
The TV continues   to   blare
   to an empty room.

©2020
(from my book **I No Longer Hear You Sing**)

A Tree Fell in the City

the streets bled   a child cried out
fear permeated the air   in a thick dark cloud

weeping of a dove could be heard
       over the roar

torment / anger / despair drifted above all hope

again and again   oceans of rampage
       washed over the city
              cleansing away daylight

old was new again / it never left
       it hid among the lies

time retells what man cannot / will not
       bending truth
              twisting it in the wind

forgotten stories / neglected truths
       wander alleyways
              overgrown with weeds

a tree fell   but no one heard it cry
       as it laid bare open
              in rivers of blood

©2020
(from my book **I No Longer Hear You Sing**)

I Live for the Hunt

I live for the hunt
chasing dreams
racing goals.
Blue haze, orange desires
never knowing the wherefore.
My fingers curl around the sun
pulling down fire from the sky.
Burning, blinding
grail of life.

I seek green
youth of dawn.
Crumpled paper holds my truth
roadway to the stars.
The scent is beyond my reach
it intoxicates me.
I follow paths
brown, gray
forever in pursuit.

©2020
(from my book **I No Longer Hear You Sing**)

In My Dream

I stood alone
watching the sun set
gold to black.
Trees fell at my touch.
In my dream
you spoke in whispers
carried away by doves.

Night lasted
seven years times ten
to bring me here,
wandering through dark chasms.
Morning painted
the sky with your smile.
I waited.

©2020
(from my book **I No Longer Hear You Sing**)

Her Story

She was a story
she was never real
she played with paper and strings
building cities on mountaintops
cardboard skyscrapers reached the moon

She was wisdom
or so she thought
carrying dreams in a bag of green silk
woven with tears from the lake
that she walked upon each day

Telling her visions
to all that would listen
she believed the words that she spoke
floating down from the precipice
that she built
she faded into herself

©2020
(from my book **I No Longer Hear You Sing**)

Chapter 15

The Lane is a River
and other short stories
2021

pen & ink illustration by Ann Christine Tabaka, reduced in size

The Fire Eater

The forests were burning, and nothing could be done to stop it. All hope seemed lost. Day turned into night as thick black clouds of smoke blocked out the sun. Days turned into weeks, and the fire grew in intensity. Everything was parched from lack of rain. Even the air burned.

Humankind's greed had been the cause of many disasters on this earth. The constant overuse of fossil fuels disrupting the weather patterns, and the disrespect for nature in general were among few of the reasons that the forests now burned.

The indigenous people prayed to the Great Spirit, to send down the Fire Eater to save their homes and the creatures that lived on the land. Sad and frightened, the people packed all that they could carry from their simple lodgings. They gathered together their domestic and farm animals to herd with them. They needed to move to safer ground, up to the high mountains where the fire had not yet reached. There the snow-melt streams and fresh springs would keep them safe for a short while longer, but not forever if the blazes could not be contained. The mountains were too steep and rugged, and there were no roads. They would have to travel by foot and horseback, leaving all motorized vehicles behind. Sorrow filled their hearts at the thought of having to leave all that they loved.

Chilam was only 17 years old, but she was as sensitive and wise as the elders. She lived with her mother, father, three siblings and her grandmother. They had a comfortable little cabin near the edge of the woods. They farmed and raised livestock. They had the Internet, and a few other modern conveniences, but she honored the old traditions, and the beautiful handcrafts that her mother made to sell. She loved her life and would not trade it for all the money and glamour in the world. She was beyond rich in her own eyes. The stars at night were magic to her. Diamonds dancing across the velvet expanse. Where else on earth could you reach up and almost touch the Milky Way? There the sky was bluer, the water clearer, and the air purer, except for now. Now that the whole earth burned. The earth that she knew and loved was dying.

Chilam felt helpless as she assisted her family in preparation for the arduous journey ahead. She tried to remember all the beauty that her forests held, and how she would run through them playing when she was younger. She feared for her beloved forest friends, the deer, the squirrel, the mountain lion and hawk. She had named many of them over the years, and felt connected to each one of them. They were her own personal Spirit Guides. She worried; would they be able to make it out alive? She could not leave it to chance. She knew what she had to do. She would go into the woods to look for her friends, and tell them to follow her to a new home far away from the approaching flames.

The day came for the village to move. They could not wait a day longer. Chilam was nowhere to be found. Her family looked everywhere for her but could not find her. In a panic they went to the village elder to ask for a search party to help them look. The elder said it was too late and that they had to leave now or be eaten up by the flames. Her family was heartbroken, but they had other children and grandmother to care for, so they left behind a message for Chilam, for when she would come back to the village. They were sure that she would come back. She had to be safe, they had been praying so hard. The Fire Eater would come and save her.

Evening was setting in as Chilam wandered deeper into the forest. Over and over again she called out to her friends, "Tahca, Zica, Igmuwatogla." She was becoming tired and was starting to choke from all the thick smoke. She could hardly breathe when she finally sat down on a rock to rest. The rock was very warm to the touch, and she knew that was a sign that she had to leave soon or perish. She wept as she called out to the Great Spirit to save her and her animals. "Please oh Great Spirit, hear my cry and send the Fire Eater to save us." She started to grow weaker by the minute, and finally passed out. Hawk found her first, and alighted by her side. He let out a great screech to call the others. Startled, she came to. She stood to her feet, and started following beneath Hawk as he flew overhead. He would guide her to safety, she knew he would. They came to a clearing in the middle of the woods where the fire had not yet reached. There, standing before her were many of her forest friends, all huddled together in fear. No predators, no prey, just creatures trying to survive this monstrous disaster. It reminded her of an artist's images of Eden in the holy book she read as a little girl.

Suddenly, on the other side of the clearing, Chilam noticed a small trail leading away from the fire. She decided to try to lead her friends towards the mountains, where she knew her people would be going. She began singing a beautiful native song to them as she walked towards the trail. It was a song that her grandmother would sing to her whenever she was frightened as a child. The beautiful native language was soothing, as was the tune. The animals all lifted their heads to listen to the enticing melody. One by one they began to walk behind her. She had their trust. She tried to be brave, but her voice faltered as she continued with her song. She tried to imagine that she was like mighty Moses leading the chosen people across the Red Sea, away from the danger that followed them. If she could only hold on to that image in her mind, maybe she could keep her courage up.

Meanwhile, the village continued their trek, slowly snaking up the rocky mountainside. Families, elderly, infants, and the ailing, all traveling into the unknown. Each person doing whatever they could manage to try to help the other. Lifting, carrying, pushing, struggling for their lives. All, exhausted and parched from the hot air that followed them every step of the way. Hoping beyond hope that their efforts would not be in vain. Chilam's family stopped to look back. They continued to quietly chant their solemn prayer. They were very worried, but they knew if anyone could manage to defeat the elements, that Chilam would be the one to do it. There was always something special about her, something spiritual about her, something mystical. They picked up their packs and continued on with the others, leaving a trail of prayer beads along the path behind them. Hopeful breadcrumbs to be followed by their daughter.

Night fell, but it was difficult to tell the difference with all the black smoke in the atmosphere. It had been dark the whole day. The smell of charred wood was beginning to overtake everyone. Chilam and her friends could tell that the fire was growing closer as they trekked onward. The animals traveled by sheer instinct, following the only sign of hope that they had, a young woman. She was their savior. They would not stop to rest, for if they did, the fire would catch up to them. They had no choice but to keep going. In the darkness they progressed by touch, using the trees' bark like braille.

Just as daybreak tried to show itself through the thick fumes, a strange sound was heard in the distant sky. Chilam's heart raced as the sound grew louder and closer. She had heard that sound before, she was sure she knew what it was. Then out of the smoke and fire appeared several large helicopters whirling overhead. She screamed and waved her arms while jumping up and down. Hawk decided to fly higher to try to intercept. The helicopter pilot almost lost control seeing a huge Red-tailed Hawk soaring towards the craft, then continually circling it. It was if the hawk was trying to get his attention, but how can that be? The firefighters were looking down, following the flight of the hawk when they noticed a human female and a group of animals on the trail below.

Then, as large streams of water came down from the helicopters, quenching the areas around Chilam and her forest friends, she noticed one of the mechanical birds come down to land. Out jumped several firemen and firewomen, suited for their work with gas masks and protective attire. One tall man, Jorge, came running up to her as the others fought the nearby blaze. Jorge raised his mask to speak to her. He was handsome and strong looking. Their eyes met and Chilam smiled up at him. Relief flooded over her weak body as she almost collapsed into his arms. Jorge insisted that she come with him on to the helicopter, but Chilam stood firm, crossed her arms and said in a stern voice, "No, I am not leaving my friends. They need me now more than ever."

No matter how hard he argued, Jorge could not change her mind, and other than lifting her over his shoulder and forcing her aboard, he had no other choice but to join her. Chilam told him where her village was heading and asked that the firefighters go find them and bring them to safety. Jorge signaled to his copter crew to join the others and continue on in search of the villagers. Jorge was fascinated, and a bit startled at the strange array of wild animals that surrounded Chilam and seemed to be in her trust. She explained that they were all her friends and her Spirit Guides. She would never abandon them. Three of the helicopters went ahead to find and help the villagers, while one staid with the unlikely parade that was led by Chilam, and now Jorge as well. They still had a long way to go by foot.

As the weary group finally met up with the rest of the villagers, the fire was starting to be held in control, at least in certain areas. Many more fire crews had joined the original one. Dedicated men and woman from everywhere on the planet had volunteered to fight this horrific inferno. Helicopter and ground crews together worked day and night for weeks on end to contain the worst of the fire. There started to be a glimmer of hope, and the people of the village gave thanks. They would need to build new homes in a different area, but no lives were lost. The livestock and domestic animals were also safe, along with the many wild animals in Chilam's care. It would take a long time for life to return to normal, but everyone was now safe, and a thanksgiving feast was planned.

After the disaster had quieted down, and things started to return to normal, Jorge would come to visit Chilam regularly, and in time she learned that his family was from a native people in Central America, from a population related to her own people. They had many of the same beliefs and customs as her people did. Even some of their native language was similar. He too loved nature and the simple way of life. Needless to say, Chilam and Jorge fell in love, and eventually they married. Jorge grew to love all the forest creatures that he helped save. It was a beautiful relationship among all the living beings. They spent many afternoons in the forest visiting their friends together.

In the end, the villagers' prayers were answered, and it became quite evident to all, that the great "Fire Eater" could come in many forms, even as a human in a helicopter.

pen & ink illustration by Ann Christine Tabaka, , reduced in size

Tim Tang, Tam Ting, and Bik

Tim Tang and Tam Ting were two-year-old Panda Bears that were relocated from the lush green forests of the Gansu province in China, to a zoo in the eastern United States of America. They were purchased at a great price with hopes of their mating and producing young pandas. They were both healthy and beautiful specimens of their species. Their thick soft coats of white with black accents sparkled in the sunlight. When captured, they displayed all the excellent qualities that the purchasing zoo was looking for. Tam Ting was romping and playing with her sister, under her mother's watchful eyes. Tim Tang was racing other male pandas up the mountain sides competing for the tastiest bamboo plants. All of that was to change soon.

The long arduous airplane trips, while stuck in small cages, in the dark cargo holds was not very pleasant for either of them. They arrived at BMI airport in Baltimore one day apart. From the day they were first captured, everything was very strange to them; the sounds, the smells, the humans bustling all around jabbering. They were very confused, and could not understand a word that the furless ones were uttering. They wondered what was happening to them.

Tam Ting hung her head low. She was very depressed because she was taken away from her mother and sister. She did not know what she did wrong to deserve this great punishment. She moped and would not respond to any stimulus. Tim Tang was furious because he was just becoming old enough to challenge other male pandas for territory and females. He ranted and raged the entire time in his small cage. Neither panda was very happy about the situation they were thrust into. No one asked them if they wanted to leave their family and homes in the mountain forests. One day they were living a normal panda life, and the next day everything was turned upside down.

Tim Tang and Tam Ting were cordial enough when they were first introduced to each other. They calmly exchanged pleasantries, and asked where each had lived before. They even knew a few of the same panda families. Both were too distraught to be more interested in each other, so after a short but friendly chat, each walked away to seek out their own corner of the zoo's panda compound. The compound was set up with treed hills to climb, and a small spring with fresh running water. There was a large patch of ripe bamboo plants ready for munching on, and a section where more bamboo was being grown to replace the eaten plants. There was a small cave under the artificial hill that they could use for shelter. It was designed to look as closely to their native habitat as possible. But neither panda was fooled. They knew it wasn't home. They decided to plot a way to escape and return to their real home.

Many weeks passed and the pandas showed no interest in being together or mating. The zoo management and vet grew concerned. The pandas didn't fight or spat, but they just did not show an ounce of affection towards each other. They often sat in the same area, but several feet apart with their backs turned toward each other. They would occasionally turn to speak to each other out of loneliness. Tam Ting would often ask Tim Tang, "Why would they do this to us? Do they hate our kind so much as to separate us from everything that we love?" Tim Tang would just shrug and shake his head before lying down and curling up into a ball to take a nap out of boredom.

Three months passed, and winter was nearing. It was getting cold, but the pandas did not mind the cold. One day a tiny black and white tuxedo kitten came strolling in through the zoo's large black iron gates. She squeezed through easily enough. She wasn't sure where she was, or where she should go to next. She wandered around looking into all the animal pits and cages thinking to herself, "That is no way for such big magnificent animals to live." She was too frightened to try to make friends with the huge polar bears, plus their compound was too cold and icy. She said "Hello," then moved along. The tigers were too scary, even though they were feline like she was, and the bison did not look much like the friendly sort. Then she came upon the panda's compound and looked in. Tam Ting looked so sad, that the poor little kitten could not help herself. She jumped right in, sauntered up to the young panda and said "Hello, I am all alone and I would like to be your friend, if you would let me." Tam Ting sat straight up looking surprised and replied, "Who and what are you? You look like a baby panda with your black and white coloring." The kitten replied, "I am a cat. I do not know my name since my mother, brothers and sisters were captured two nights ago, but I escaped. I do not know where they are and I am cold and lonely." Tam Ting lit up and asked, "May

158

I give you a name?" The kitten thought about it for a few seconds then said, "Yes, I would be happy to have a name." Tam Ting said, "Your eyes are the color of the rare pale jade in my homeland, I will call you Bik, which means jade in my native language." "Oh, I love that name" the kitten announced, "I am Bik!" Then Tam Ting stopped to think for a moment. She said, "I am happy to cuddle with you and keep you warm, but we eat bamboo, and sometime an egg or some pumpkin as a treat. What do you need to eat?" The kitten looked pensive then said, "I am a great hunter, I will keep your home free of mice and vermin, and that shall be my food." Both seemed happy with the agreement and Bik curled up in Tam Ting's arms and they drifted off into a comfortable sleep.

The next morning when Tim Tang saw Tam Ting playing with Bik, he came over and asked, "What is this?" Tam Ting said, "This is my new friend Bik. See her beautiful eyes, the color of our native jade." Tim Tang asked, "Will you be my friend too?" Bik jumped up into his arms and started to purr loudly. The three new friends romped and cuddled and had so much fun.

Later that morning, all the visitors to the zoo crowded around the exhibit excitingly taking photos. When one of the employees saw what was happening, they sent for the zoo's vet. The vet came immediately with her technician. They cautiously entered the compound and approached the pandas and the kitten. They were concerned that the pandas might harm the kitten, but when they got nearer, they noticed that Tam Ting was lovingly holding the kitten and it was purring. The vet tried to take the kitten, but her technician tapped her on the shoulder, and said, "Look how happy they seem. Tam Ting and the kitten both look as if they are pleading with their eyes, and Tim Tang is standing defensively behind them." The vet nodded and decided to try talking to the animals. "May I please take the kitten for a little while, to make sure she is healthy?" The pandas did not understand her words, but the vet's voice sounded kind and her facial expression was loving, so they handed the kitten over to the vet. The Vet said, "Well. I suppose we will need to find a name for you, won't we? How about Sun Li?" All three animals looked disapprovingly. Then the vet tried several more Chinese names. None of them seemed to make the animals happy. Finally, she exclaimed, "AHA, bright jade eyes, I know, how about Bik?" The kitten smiled and meowed loudly. "So, Bik it is" replied the vet, then she added, "Let's take you back to the hospital to get you checked on, and up on all your vaccinations. Meanwhile my tech will go out to get you some proper cat food and nice warm cat bed to sleep in."

Bik washappy and felt right at home with her new family, even though their habits were very different from hers. She loved to snuggle with Tam Ting, and she would race up the trees with Tim Tang chasing after her, all in fun of course. Meanwhile Tim Tang and Tam Ting became more affectionate towards each other, and started to spend an unusual amount of time together. The vet and other panda experts never experienced a male-female relationship such as this before. Usually males will mate, then move on, but this pair seemed to become a true couple. The vet wondered if Bik had something to do with it.

The vet kept a close eye on Tam Ting, and started to notice signs that she was pregnant. The zoo owners and the vet decided to start making a list of possible names for the expected cub. One day the vet came into the compound to check on Tam Ting, and of course Bik was right there by her side, watching everything that was going on. The vet had learned that even though she and the pandas could not speak the same language, they were able to communicate quite adequately by observing each other's facial expressions and body language. Then of course Bik would always chime in vocally as if she was translating for the pandas. The vet started to read off names for the baby panda. Both Tam Ting and Bik seemed uninterested until she said "Ling-Ling." Both Tam Ting and Bik sat up erect with their ears perked up. They seemed to smile as they looked at each other and nodded. Yes, the vet was amazed, but they actually nodded at each other. Then they both turned towards her in unison and nodded again. "Well, I guess that is it then. The baby's name will be Ling-Ling" the vet responded. She walked away wondering if what just happened really did happen.

Five months later a tiny female baby panda was born. Tam Ting was a very proud and devoted mother, and kept Ling-Ling safely hidden from the public at first. The vet and her technician checked in on the family several times each day. When Ling-Ling was ready to come out into the compound, she became the star attraction of the zoo. Hordes of visitors would gather around the panda compound to see little Ling-Ling and her parents. But, the biggest attraction of all was the strange little nanny. Bik was constantly with little Ling-Ling, grooming her and carefully guarding her, like any good nanny would do.

scratchboard illustration by Ann Christine Tabaka, reduced in size

Chapter 16

Learning to Climb the Mountain
2022

Another Day, Another Year

The wind cries / I do not listen. You hold out your hand
one last time. Startled, a fox runs under the Clethra.
Clouds fill a darkened sky. I am soaked with a deluge
of tears. Mud collects at my knees. Where has the fox
gone? Needles pierce my soul, releasing blue desires.
Awash in a dream of yesterday / you never planned to stay.
I rip open my chest & tear out my heart. It washes away
with the storm / lost downstream. Another day, another
year.It might have been so different. The fox cries out,
I follow.

©2022
(from my book **Learning to Climb the Mountain**)

*Nominated for the **2023 Dwarf Stars award of the
Science Fiction and Fantasy Poetry Association**

Learning to Climb the Mountain

I read a book once: *The Fear of Flying*.
It was not about flying at all.
I climbed a mountain,
spread my wings and tried to soar.
The cat thought I was crazy
as I tumbled to the ground.
I was twenty then.
I did not know my power yet.

Life lingered on the cusp,
the old man shed his beard.
Tides ran their rhythms with the moon.
I idled away my life in snips and dreads,
always going the wrong way,
then doubling back.
I was forty then,
still turning pages to discover who I was.

I visited a Greek Garden once.
It was not in Greece.
I rushed home
to plant my seeds among the thorns.
The sparrows were dismayed
that Doric columns did not grow.
I was too old then.
Too many years had crumbled beneath my feet.

(from my book **Learning to Climb the Mountain**)

She Painted the Sky Orange
An Ode to Georgia Totto O'Keeffe

I remember reading about her when
I was in school. Her passion filled me
with a fire that I never knew before.

She knew her calling at age ten.
Wisconsin, Illinois, New York, Texas,
she devoured them all. New Mexico stole her heart.

Broken love, broken spirit, clear vision,
she claimed the world as her own. She saw
impressions of a future that were rooted in the past.

Skyscrapers morphing into mountains.
Painted landscapes playing in pure light.
Cosmic flowers opening to desire.

Devotions of a sacred desert spoken
in bleached white bones. She was an
evolving canvas of raw emotion.

She reached up to touch the sky once,
bewitching it to sing in orange.
You cannot see what you cannot touch.

Her brush wrote across a canvas of imagination,
telling stories that could not be told in words.
Vivid images of another world.

She forged the way to modernism for women.
A new way to look at the world,
through vibrant colored eyes.

It was because of her, and others like her,
that I began to explore who I was.
I want to paint the sky orange.

©2022
(from my book **Learning to Climb the Mountain**)

watercolor painting of "Daylilies"
converted to B&W image by Ann Christine Tabaka, reduced in
size

Dashboard Jesus

It was an era of the car chapel. Rosary hanging
from rear-view mirror / Saint Christopher medal,
complete with glove-compartment prayer book.
Magnetic Sacred Heart statue on the dashboard.

Mother was devout. I was fourteen. Life was cold.
She was fifty when she learned to drive,
after my father's disease took him. A sorrowful
blessing. Jesus would show us the way / take care of us.

Her first car / a blue cracker-box / Renault.
it gave her new freedom. Saturday confession.
Sunday Mass. Weekdays reserved for work.
Dashboard Jesus kept his promise. He watched over us.

I was twenty-two,that night.
My son was eighteen months. Darkness and sleet partnered
to do their worst. She worked late / did not come home.
Phone ringing off the hook. It was the police / I knew.

Inebriated / he backed down the on-ramp / lights off.
He was unharmed. Twisted metal and blood-filled
highway. They pried my mother out. A long night
at the hospital. I learned to pray / I dared to hope.

Mom's car accordioned / she survived. When finally
conscious, she said "go to the car." The ravage
was complete. Floating upon water and blood was a
plastic box / tiny baby moccasins / there where she said.

On the dashboard stood that statue / staring down at me.
I can never forget that day. After months of surgeries,
my mother recovered. My son wore the moccasins.
I began to understand her devotion. I shed my disbelief
like skin. Dashboard Jesus Saves!

©2022
(from my book **Learning to Climb the Mountain**)

colored ink illustration converted to B&W by Ann Christine
Tabaka, reduced in size

He Flies His Cage

I have no idea how birds fly. I cannot see their wings
beat past my own gaze. Nor do I feel the air flow of
soft feathers on the wind. I have no idea how a child
becomes what it is not. He left my womb too long ago.
I cannot see his future / grappling with false faith.
He flew away beyond my reach. I am torn in two / feathers
scattered far & wide. A gale escapes my withered lungs.
Wings clipped / I am grounded. I have not gotten there yet,
to that place between life and death. I tried so many times,
in so many ways. I am not as strong as I used to be. I used
to be strong. Life has a way of snatching our dreams
before we are done playing with them. I do not exist
anymore. I am just a shadow left behind in the wilderness.

©2022
(from my book **Learning to Climb the Mountain**)

Anna

The ocean bore her seven times, upon its rolling spine.
Storms could not unfold her / a sister to the angry waves.
She lived ninety-seven years among the clouds, not
knowing how to rain. Decades carried buckets, waiting
for a tear. She was too stubborn to cry. I remember
furrowed brow / deep valleys east to west. Determined,
she would not cleave. Three children lost, two survived.
Yet, one would take his life. She was stone & iron. She
could not be broken / refused to rust. There was a time
when she was soft, before I held her hand. Her stories
nourished my need. She gave what she could not receive.
I watched her brow soften as she knelt to say goodbye.
A lifetime of tears flooded out to wash away the pain.

©2022(from my book **Learning to Climb the Mountain**)

Anna, my Barcia / Grandmother, circa 1927

I Hear the Water

I hear the water.
It calls to me from lakes, and streams, and rivers.

My mother was the ocean.
She carried me on her shoulders above raging storms.

Her strength washed away islands, eroding sin.
Dolphins swam in her dreams and gulls sang of her glory.

I walk on water.
I am her child, the one she bore in sorrow.

Man raped her bounty, polluted her shores,
but still, she did not cry.

I am rain.
I will cry for her.

©2022
(from my book Learning to Climb the Mountain)

Lost Summers of my Youth

The sweetness of summer, falling from trees /
ripe / soft / luscious dreams of forever.
We were the ones who begged at street corners,
never bowing our heads. Church baskets on
back porches / filled with tomorrow's hope.
Steaming blacktop and <melting> tar / strong
odors of everyday life. Mama worked 2 jobs /
we lived by latchkey. Freedom / a timeless
concept, it wafted above the gray steam. Ice
Cream Truck songs calling to youthful joy / with
never a dime for a cone. Bookmobiles carrying
wonderous worlds of fantasy / we lived for Saturday
afternoons. Looking back - to be poor was to be rich.
We needed so little / we wanted so much.
Hand-me-down lives that reached for the stars.
Summer will never be the same.

©2022
(from my book **Learning to Climb the Mountain**)

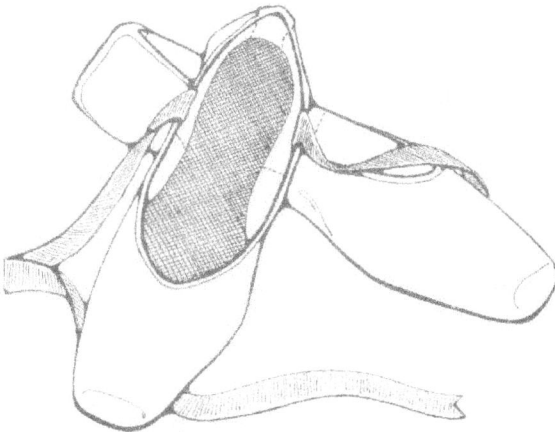

sketch by Ann Christine Tabaka, reduced in size

Memories in the Key of C

I have my own pages
grasped in aging hands.
Words wander through the course
      drifting off the edge.

We were wayward souls - you and I,
      before our bodies touched.

Sweet fragrance of night
wrapped us in its love

I savor the past
      held in little cups
served up neatly
      upon a king-sized bed

      In the distance,
         a bell
         tolled
      Lavender tunes sprang
         from
         our
         lips

The exquisite pain of morning
      when you walked away

Searching for lost words
I am a broken song

©2022
(from my book **Learning to Climb the Mountain**)

Too Much / Too Much

lost beneath a colorful *storm*
umbrellaed rooftops
        tent-city streets

sheltered from *incessant* rain
weary   lost   fragmented
        footsteps slosh through time

heavens release a *deluge* of tears
drowning words of *indignation*
        seeking a dry home

debris flooded gutters
        a [swirling] river of *myriad* sins

blank stares reflect
        on dancing puddles
pocked with *heavy* downpour

a *thousand* tiny deaths took hold
as I looked [beneath] the *maelstrom*
        for you

sun   reprieve   all motion stops
        umbrellas fold

faces lift towards clearing skies
        busy streets continue on
            [without you]

©2022
(from my book **Learning to Climb the Mountain**)

Passing Moons

There is something beautiful
     about the way you walk,
faltering yet so lithe.
Ten-thousand moons have passed us by,
     since we parted ways.

We sat up all night talking about ocean creatures,
     and mystical places we have been.
We touched a realm of emotions never felt before.

     first one
     then two
     then seven
visions cast upon the sea.

We made our way towards reunion,
     forgetting all lost hope.

Looking back,
there was no more that could have been done.
Now you walk away once more,
     faltering yet so lithe,
while another moon is about to rise.

©2022
(from my book **Learning to Climb the Mountain**)

Best Friends Interrupted

You were petals upon my rose / I was thorns
You were the best of me.
You = balance / me = chaos,
[together] we made gray.

[Interlocking] pieces of some perfect plan,
hopscotching over any problems,
righting any wrongs.

Time did its worst to tear us,
we could not be torn.
Aging photographs and mementoes
filled our treasure chest.

One miscalculation ended
that which could not be foreseen.
The day that death did
what no one else could do …
interrupted us.

©2022
(from my book **Learning to Climb the Mountain**)

Chapter 17

Children of the Storm
2022

pen & ink illustration by Ann Christine Tabaka, reduced in size

Guarded Truths

Your first step was a leap,
your first word a proclamation.
You were brilliance before your time.
Years have shielded the truth,
you were never meant to be.
A timeless lie, drifting above ocean waves.
Words sinking below the surface.
Summers came and summers went.
You were always so precocious.
A wily fox, ripe for the hunt,
fur gleaming in the sun.
My beautiful boy.
Truth washed ashore,
drifting sands now rule your future.
You can no longer fear
what could never be told.
Your secret dies with me.

©2022
(from my book **Children of the Storm**)

Remembering That Night

That was the night I climbed a hill,
searching for answers. Questions
stuck in my throat. I found you
standing there, starlight glistening
in your eyes. A flock of geese
flew past the moon. We sat and talked
'til dawn, sharing stories of the
empress and the thief. Promises
were made.

Winter stretched across the land.
Clouds blocked out the sun.
Answers never came. Sipping
jasmine tea & honey, stories
grew cold. Once upon a times,
now fading with the years.
We went our separate ways.
I hold on to memories that
once glistened with the stars.

©2022
(from my book **Children of the Storm**)
* Nominated for the **2023 Pushcart Prize in Poetry**
      (by *Sequoyah Cherokee River Journal*)

Eclipse

Diana, ruler of the night sky, slowly
rises above the dune line. Sounds of
crashing waves applaud her arrival.
The heavens glow under her beauty.
She smiles. Earth's shadow gently
kisses her cheek. And so, it begins.
A tryst that lasts for hours. She
vanishes under his cloak. Piece by
piece she is consumed by his lust.
A hazy crimson blush covers her
countenance. Blackness expands
above, every star sings out in
triumph. Diamonds dance across
the firmament. The shadow leisurely
retreats. It is finished.

©2022
(from my book **Children of the Storm**)

Liquid Sky

Searing heat rises in agonizing waves,
eating away at sanity.
Rippled air drips down,
choking out all breath.

Refracted images dance
across parched land.
Summer an inferno,
swallowing fragile lives.

Deniers will deny!

Grass … brown … scorched & curled.
Wilting flora cries out begging for rain.
Birds refuse to fly.

Countries burn
Hearts stop
People die

The old folk tell of past canicules,
but none this tortuous.
A fevered sky stretches on
with no relief in sight.

Memories of balmy days waft in and out,
as mercury soars.
A liquid sky melts down
upon abarren earth.

©2022
(from my book **Children of the Storm**)

When Dreams Wither

There is some deep meaning hidden within.
Egg shells crack open spilling desires. No one
told me how to pray. Last year's nest is dry.
I hold it in my trembling hands, searching for
answers. Truth is a festering of blowflies,
sucking life from my womb. I am old and
forgotten. Barren. Parts of me crumble into
dust. The willow nods. Leaves shower down as
I place the nest gently on the ground. She folds
her branched arms in on me. We weep.

©2022
(from my book **Children of the Storm**)

pen & ink illustration by Ann Christine Tabaka, reduced in size

Time Has Passed Away

Time has passed away,
like the dead dandelions
that drift upon a breeze.

It floats above our fallen dreams
like some specter from film noir.

You hold out your hand,
but all feeling is lost.
Numbness sets in.

We bury the mantel clock
as a symbol of all things forgotten.

Once we knew how to sing.
Our voices now crack like lightning.
A sharp, raspy requiem pours out.

Youth is undervalued,
we play with it so carelessly.
All that is left is a faded photograph,
of who we once were.

Burial over, we stand up,
brushing the dirt from our knees,
and say goodbye to time.

©2022
(from my book **Children of the Storm**)

Bayside

The perfect evening … rolling waves gently kiss the shore.
Dancing moonglow hypnotizing the senses. We walk hand
in hand in moist marsh grass, birds scattering in our wake.
Magic fills the air. The softness of forever held in a solitary
moment. Daylight drips down from a lavender sky. Night
takes over as the starry curtain falls. Sounds echo off a
distant shore. Stillness surrounds. Quietude!

You once loved me on a night like this. Time has a way
of remembering such things. You are the one who taught
me that one plus one could equal much more than two, and
that a lifetime could exist in a single breath. A cool breeze
sings across the bay. Tucking the stars into our dreams,
we turn to walk towards dawn. No words are spoken.

©2022
(from my book **Children of the Storm**)

Slow Dancing with Time

The time I visited you and you lost your way,
there was snow on the ground.
Red berries glistened on holly trees
while robins gorged themselves.
Time had no meaning.

You stared out the window.
I held your hand.
Looking at me, you asked, "Why?"
I had no answer then, only prayers.

Each day another small death
repeating the doleful dance.

Weeks passed; months passed … a year.

It was winter again.
A year felt like ten.
There were no holly trees where you were.
No feasting robins.

You looked at me and asked me, "Who?"
I leaned over to whisper, "Your daughter."
Your eyes smiled, but you did not.
Some faint memory stirred, then faded.

Another year passed.
A flock of robins flew overhead.
I stood in the snow
while placing a holly branch upon your grave.

©2022
(from my book **Children of the Storm**)

As Moon Beams Fade

The tiger prowls at night,
hunting moon beams as its prey.
Wandering apparitions sail the darkness,
searching for a place to rest.
Landing past dawn,
they evaporate with the sunrise.
Streaks of red paint the imagination.
We look beyond our own sight.
Stories once told to children
no longer find a home.
What is real and what is not
are questions for the ages.
We cannot hold on to dreams
that perish in the light.
Time does not belong to us.
Wisdom has its worth.
We pack our bags and walk away,
never looking back,
as moon beams fade before our eyes.

©2022
(from my book **Children of the Storm**)

The Monkey Danced a Polka

The monkey danced a Polka. No one wants to take
 my hand. I am lost to the busy *streets, lanes, roads,*
 highways of life. I watch as birds fly by, dropping feathers
on the crowd. Streetcar bells clang out calling passengers
to their stop. No one sees me standing there - alone and
lonely, I climb on board. The ghosts of disemboweled
dreams haunt my thoughts. Where did I see that face
before? Everywhere I look, a circus of humanity. Time is
an illusion placed in ajar upon a shelf. I remember seeing
it there, pushed towards the back. I feel the pressure of
distant mountains, as they topple to the shore. The monkey
plays with the jar, letting time escape. The music stops.
Passengers disembark. After the dance is over,
how does one tie up loose ends?

©2022
(from my book **Children of the Storm**)

The Last Songbird

Gone to history are the birds that sing,
mouths open wide to swallow the sun.
Pasting together pieces of lost time, as
daylight dissolves into night. As a child
I plucked feathers from my wounds /
wounds inflicted by the beast. A tangle
of limbs. Tender ligaments stretched
beyond capacity. I limped into a future
where hope did not exist. There I found
absolution from my sins. Pain could not
stop me from my quest.
I must find the last songbird!

©2022
(from my book **Children of the Storm**)

Winter Dreams

Winter tires waiting for spring, as I tire of life.
A sky of slate overshadows the day.

I am tar, once blistered by searing heat,
now cracked and scarred by the cold.

Ancient stars burn out
while singing lullabies to nebulae.
Time fades from existence in a single breath.

Hoping, dreaming, yearning, we saunter past dawn.
Some things never change. Why do we go in circles?

Darkness calls us into the storm.
The struggle becomes the path.

Spring is forever gone.
I have lived too long to remember the warmth.
Winter is here to stay.

©2022
(from my book **Children of the Storm**)

Chapter 18

How Do You Uncook an Egg?
2024

watercolor painting of "Tulips"
converted to B&W image by Ann Christine Tabaka, reduced in
size

Waiting to be Saved

Time walked off … taking me by the hand.
She knew my struggles - all too well.
Not everyone will understand.
I was alone again / even with you there.

Devoid of dreams / devoid of love,
I took a walk.

Lost to myself / I traversed a woodland trail.
Approaching the stream / there stood a covered
bridge / stripped naked. Its lattice bared like an
immense wooden screen. Peering through its
skeletal frame / I knew how it felt. Exposed
to the elements / exposed to life.
Barren and forsaken.
Waiting to be saved.

Light was fading / I knew what I must do.
I continued on. But now it was I who took time
by the hand … showing her the way home.

©2024
(from my book **How do You Uncook an Egg?**)

There Can Never be Another Casablanca

There can never be another *Casablanca*. There
can only be one epic drama / one epic romance.
Some sagas can be retold /rewritten, but this one
cannot. No one will ever replace the actors with
such immortal style. Years in the making / hours
to observe. *Romeo & Juliet* – it is not! I need
your succor / the enemy nears. Darkness overcomes
dusk / time explodes in sparks & flares / battle has
begun. We never stop fighting / we never stop
learning / we never give in to fear. *Morrocco* /
land of mystery & romance - there love stories
go to die. I close my eyes to destruction and war.
I march to the song in my dream. And yet … time
vanishes too quickly. I waited for too long / the
curtain begins to fall.
La Marseillaise starts to play.

©2024
(from my book **How do You Uncook an Egg?**)

Tuna Salad Sandwich Dreams

Tuna salad dreams fly overhead.
Hunger sets in. Childhood memories –
steamy bowls of canned tomato soup &
white bread sandwiches, crusts cut off –
soft & squishy. The warmth of youth,
when life was simpler. Checkered sheets
& floral print towels, an era from past pages.
Stories written in a lined black marbled
notebook with a leaky fountain pen.
Poems written in hope / words full of life.
Resonate!
Hand-me-down clothes & second-hand dreams.
Walking backwards through a lintel of lost time.
Craving a taste of the past / I walk into the
kitchen to prepare a tuna salad dream.

©2024
(from my book **How do You Uncook an Egg?**)

watercolor paintingconverted to B&W image by Ann Christine
Tabaka, reduced in size

The Soul Has No Gender

pronouns – do not a person make / the
soul has no gender. cells divide & cells
combine – to form a body whole. whatever
physicality lives within our structure is not
the final product. we grow & evolve / we
move & expand / we are never concrete.
the ocean is not he nor she. we come from
earth & so we return / we are elemental
beings. thus, do not judge – for judgement
owns the final hour. emotions rule, appearances
fade / only time can claim our path. tread
carefully my friend. life speaks to us in many
colors. pronouns – do not a person make / in
the end only one rule holds true -
love and be loved.

©2024
(from my book **How do You Uncook an Egg?**)

Charade

I've lost my way – among the brambles of life,
pricked by thorns of indecision. I am the *unsung*,
the *unloved*, the *forgotten* … to each penny a
thought is paid. Stray desires pursue an illusion.
The moon hides its face & stars refuse to shine.
Autumn calls to me. I have learned to cry
in silence, to hold back the flood of despair.
Sadness crushes the night, leaving shards of
dreams in its path. Long-winded words join
short-sighted actions to complete the charade.
I must pick up the pieces of my broken past &
learn to live without you. I cannot pretend anymore.

©2024
(from my book **How do You Uncook an Egg?**)

Aurora

I want to feel the dancing waves of light & bathe in
a shimmeringheaven. To hear the sparks of Aurora
as she sings her lullaby. Greens & blues surround each
word - vibrations reach ever higher. I want to partake
in the song of gods, not meant for mortals. She demands
only that we believe. Footsteps of time, pace across
a frozen tundra. We hold on to truths that cannot die.
Magic paints reality upon a canvas of imagination.
Take me in your arms and carry me to a realm of wonder.
I am where I am meant to be. One dream among a
thousand sets flight. I am home.

©2024
(from my book **How do You Uncook an Egg?**)

Sunrise Holds Memories

I walk past dawn – feet sinking deep in wet sand.
Salt air fills my senses. Thunderous sound of crashing
waves echo in my head. Southpoint is empty this time
of day - it is mine to absorb. The tide rolls out carrying
expectations on its shoulders. Sunrise holds memories.
I climbed a mountain once – in the Colorado Rockies.
Air thin as a noon shadow - Mt. Sneffles towered above
clouds. Ice axes and canteens escaped, racing down
cliffside along with my dreams. So much snow – the
memory brings a chill on this abandoned day. I become
lost in *faces, places*, *&events* that swirl like an eddy
caught beneath the pier. Sunlight makes its entrance.
Beach glass & tumbled shells sparkle in delight. Images
recede – memories are tucked back into a locked
box of time. The sun touches my face & I walk off
to meet my future – dawn following in my footsteps.

©2024
(from my book **How do You Uncook an Egg?**)

Racing Dreams

Dreams of racing above clouds haunt my past.
Peering down on fearsome foes.
As a child I would wake with a start - still
breathless from the chase.
Dizzying images of trees swirled beneath
my running feet - furiously trying to stay aloft.
Exhausted – heart pounding / drenched in sweat.
I pulled the covers over my head – hiding
from myself. Trying to make sense of what
felt so real – yet was an illusion.
Years walked pass / first slowly / then faster.
Ages sped by in a dust storm of misaligned events.
The dreams became less frequent, but persisted.
It has been years since I had this dream / still
I cannot shake it. It follows me into old age.
Aching limbs trying to race from some perceived
harm. What does it all mean? I run from myself /
I never catch up. I race my dreams to the end.
I fear - falling to earth will be my final dream.

©2024
(from my book **How do You Uncook an Egg?**)

She Was Twilight

She lived among the shadows,
sheltered from all light.
A complexity of being,
beyond known thought.
Night called her name.
Shewalked outside,
reaching for the moon,
wrapping herself in its glow,
she tiptoed across starlight.
Dreams were her only companion
as she wandered past midnight.
She saw things that no one else could,
and spoke words no one could hear.
Reality drew a curtain around her,
hiding her from fears.
She could not be owned,
she could not be tamed.
She was Twilight.

©2024
(from my book **How do You Uncook an Egg?**)

It Was Never Easy

Large white tiles – with diagonal cracks
cover the floor of my dreams.
Ants scurrying up walls
and clogged visions surround my reality.
I cannot hear music / I cannot speak words,
as night takes over the day.

reaching for a memory – life rushes by
leaving me behind.

It's not easy …
It never was easy.
Denying a past that never existed.
Fly specked summers painted on a canvas of dreams.
Lemonade afternoons.

Songs sung out of tune /
chapters written out of order /
memories askew.
Life holds out its hand to pull me in.
Past events mutate into fantasy …
people, places & things rearrange.
A fabricated youth of my own design.

The more I try to remedy it – the worse it breeds.
Apologies made – the lie remains,
embedded deep in scarred wounds.
How do you un-tell a lie?
How do you un-cook an egg?

©2024
(from my book **How do You Uncook an Egg?**)

colored ink illustration converted to B&W by Ann Christine
Tabaka, reduced in size

A Message from the Author

My life is a chaotic mosaic. It has never turned out as I had planned or expected it to. I still have no idea how I got to where I am today.

I was born to poor parents who were first generation Americans. My father was brought up in war-torn Poland until he was 15 years old. I was taunted and made fun of my entire youth. I had no idea what I was going to become, nor did I care.

I was a Tom-boy until my teens. It was then I decided I loved to draw and create. I took every art class I could in high school and went to the local college as an arts major. I wanted to be an artist and a dress designer. The 60's happened, and I "dropped out." I married young and had one son. I needed to support my son. I learned that I was good at math and science, so I started working at the DuPont Experimental Station in an Organic Chemistry Lab. I worked my way up and took classes. I became a Senior Staff Scientist. My art fell by the wayside since chemistry made more money than art did. Although I did have a semi-successful art career on the side. I sold most of what I painted and illustrated.

I have had 3 husbands (I am still with number 3), and several careers along the way. After I retired from being an organic chemist, I went to school and became nationally certified as a personal trainer.

Over the years I always scribbled down rhymes and musings in note books. Luckily, I kept most of them. I was never good at English Lit, spelling, or grammar, so how I started to compose poems and short stories is beyond me. But here I am today.

This book is a sort of "Master Works" of my favorite writing, art work and photography. Thank you for joining me on my journey!

Ann Christine Tabaka

P.S. All of the artwork in this book has been reduced from full size paintings and illustrations. My illustrations were 16" X 22" and my paintings were 22" X 28".

scratchboard illustration by Ann Christine Tabaka, reduced in size

About The Author

Ann Christine Tabaka was nominated for the 2017& 2023 Pushcart Prize in Poetry; nominated for the 2023 Dwarf Stars award of the Science Fiction and Fantasy Poetry Association; winner of Spillwords Press 2020 Publication of the Year; selected as a Judge for the Soundwaves Poetry Contest of Northern Ireland 2023. Her bio is featured in the "Who's Who of Emerging Writers 2020" and "2021," published by Sweetycat Press. She is the author of 17 poetry books, and 1 short story book, and has been published widely in National & International journals and magazines. She lives in Delaware, USA. She loves gardening and cooking. Chris lives with her husband and four cats.

www.ingramcontent.com/pod-product-compliance
Lightning Source LLC
Chambersburg PA
CBHW051421090426
42737CB00014B/2766